I have very much enjoyed Steph
sporting world, both from the an
and from the high-level professional elite sports people.
I would love a dollar for every time I've been asked how, as a Christian, I navigated the world of international rugby and all that goes with it. When I was selected to play for my country at the age of 21, reading a book like *The Good Sporting Life* would certainly have helped!

I often think about the highs and lows that sport can deliver, and the pitfalls that can await a known sportsperson strutting their stuff on the global stage. These are made so much more difficult without a deep, personal relationship with God, Jesus, and the Holy Spirit to guide and provide peace and joy in all circumstances—which makes the repeated encouragement throughout this book to "Seek first his kingdom and his righteousness" one of its most helpful and important features.

Forty years after accepting the salvation that Jesus offers freely to all, I can say that my Christian relationship is the most important thing for me as I head into what is probably the final third of my life. I encourage all young sports players to learn from the wisdom found in these pages, so that they can say the same.

Nick Farr-Jones
Former captain, Australian rugby team

I'm going to order numerous copies of this book, because I stand on the touchline every week with parents who aren't near church but who love their kids, love the game, and are longing for a map with which to navigate the world of sport. I'll say to them: "This isn't really written for you, but you'd be mad not to read it." On page after page they'll find a great passion for sport, some of their heroes being quoted—and the wisdom of Scripture. I loved the read and so will they.

Rico Tice
Senior Minister, All Souls Langham Place, London

What a great read! Stephen's book is founded on a strong biblical theology with heartwarming anecdotes from Christians deeply embedded in the world of sport. This is a marvellous model of practical theology, and a work that I highly recommend.

Graham Daniels
General Director, Christians in Sport (UK)

As a first grade player, international '7s' referee and elite sports chaplain, I've found that the hardest question for Christian sportspeople hasn't been "How do I make that vital tackle?" or "How do I get the ball into the goal?" but "How do I survive as a Christian in the sporting world?" Stephen Liggins has written a book I have waited a lifetime for. It answers questions the Christian sports participant, coach, supporter and pastor want answered about Christianity and sport. It is a must-read.

Rev. Dr David Tyndall
International sports chaplain and founding member of Sports Chaplaincy Australia

THE GOOD SPORTING LIFE

Loving and playing sport as a Christian

STEPHEN LIGGINS

SYDNEY • YOUNGSTOWN

The Good Sporting Life
© Stephen Liggins 2020

All rights reserved. Except as may be permitted by the Copyright Act, no part of this publication may be reproduced in any form or by any means without prior permission from the publisher. Please direct all copyright enquiries and permission requests to the publisher.

Matthias Media
(St Matthias Press Ltd ACN 067 558 365)
Email: info@matthiasmedia.com.au
Internet: www.matthiasmedia.com.au
Please visit our website for current postal and telephone contact information.

Matthias Media (USA)
Email: sales@matthiasmedia.com
Internet: www.matthiasmedia.com
Please visit our website for current postal and telephone contact information.

Scripture taken from the Holy Bible, NEW INTERNATIONAL VERSION®, NIV®. Copyright © 1973, 1978, 1984, 2011 by Biblica, Inc. All rights reserved worldwide. Used by permission.

ISBN 978 1 925424 64 5

Cover design by Georgia Condie.
Typesetting by Lankshear Design.

CONTENTS

	Introduction	5
1.	**Playing by the book** *What the Bible says about sport*	15
2.	**Past and present** *The history of Christianity and sport*	35
3.	**The Christian sportsperson** *Living with and for God on and off the field*	55
4.	**The joy of sport** *Sport's intrinsic value*	73
5.	**Sportsmanship in an unsporting world** *Sport and good character*	93
6.	**The sports field as mission field** *Sport and outreach*	113
7.	**Sport and support** *Sport and spiritual encouragement*	139
8.	**But there's more…** *The potential benefits of good health and travel*	155

9. The sport cycle 169
   Starting out, getting serious, finishing up...
   and beyond

10. A word for... 187
    parents, coaches, referees, chaplains,
    ministers and spectators

11. A word about... 209
    sport on Sundays, praying for victory,
    how much sport, and sports ministry

Conclusion 227

Acknowledgements 229

About the author 231

INTRODUCTION

**For everything God created is good,
and nothing is to be rejected
if it is received with thanksgiving…
(1 Timothy 4:4)**

///

I watched the ball climbing higher and higher into the sky. As I did so, I realized this was the sort of thing I'd want to tell my grandchildren about one day.

It was a sunny Sydney summer's afternoon, and I was playing cricket for my club side against a formidable team from another part of the city. The opposing line-up was extremely strong and boasted the twins Stephen and Mark Waugh. Steve had been a regular member of the Australian cricket team for five years, and Mark had played his first game for the national side a few weeks earlier. Both would go on to become superstars of the game. Given the quality of our opposition, the Saturday crowd was larger than usual for a Sydney first grade fixture. Most, no doubt, had come wanting to see their national heroes in action.

Mid-afternoon on the first day of the match I was (somewhat surprisingly) batting well. I had reached 45 when the opposition captain threw the ball to Steve. We'd played together in some representative sides when younger and had gotten along well, but he was highly competitive and not the sort to hand out favours to opposing batsmen! Anticipating what was to come, I was on high alert.

As Steve ran into bowl, I knew he'd try to dominate me from the start. A first-ball bouncer was high on the list of possibilities. Sure enough, that's exactly what he delivered. As the ball reared up towards my head, I moved into position for a hook shot and swung as hard as I could. As much by accident as by design, I struck the ball perfectly in the sweet spot of the bat. Time slowed down as I watched the ball going up... up... and away. It didn't just clear the fence at the edge of the field; it went 30 or 40 metres further and brought up my half century.[1]

We've all had these golden moments in sport. But, to present a more complete picture, I should mention that a few minutes after hitting Steve out of the ground, he got me out. I *did* then re-turn the tables later in the day by dismissing him for next to nothing, but I have to admit that it was more a question of Steve playing a bad shot than me bowling a good ball. And then another opposition player absolutely smashed me (and everyone else) all over the park so that the other

---

[1] To help North American readers—cricket is a little like baseball, Steve Waugh is like a top-level Major League pitcher, a bouncer is like a beanball (except that it is a legal part of the game), and hitting the ball out of the field on the full is a little like hitting a home run, except that in cricket you can hit the ball in any direction. (As a right-hander, my shot went to the left of third base.)

team finished the day on top. Within a few hours, I went from being superstar to superdud. A few days later, Steve and Mark were off to the West Indies with the Australian side, and I was catching the train into the city for another week of work. The highs and lows of sport!

That summer, our team went on to win the Sydney first grade premiership—something that ranks as one of the highlights of my sporting life. In the years that followed, two players from that team—Adam Gilchrist and Phil Emery—went on to play for Australia, and a number of others played state cricket. I played about ten seasons for the club, had a lot of fun, suffered my fair share of injuries, and made a lot of good friends. At times I found myself in discussions of a spiritual nature, and one year myself and another bloke from the club put on a midweek *Christianity Explained* course for any of our cricketing colleagues who were interested. About five guys attended. The years have rolled by, but to this day I keep in contact with many of my former teammates.

The love of sport

Like so many others, I love playing sport—the physical challenge, the mental test, the thrill of competition, the feel of performing an athletic movement well, the satisfaction of contributing to a smoothly functioning team, the break it provides from other aspects of life, and particularly the time spent with teammates and opponents. There is something about struggling with and against others in a sporting contest that is hugely bonding.

But I don't just love playing sport. I love watching it, reading about it, and talking about it. When I was a boy, I collected the autographs of sportspeople, and even constructed complex sporting encounters with my toys on the floor at home. And I am far from alone. Sport is loved by billions of people around the world. Travel to the remotest locations on the planet and you will probably see someone wearing a Manchester United top, some kids playing with a ball, or groups of people huddled around television sets watching the football, basketball, cricket, kabaddi (look it up!), or whatever other athletic encounter you may care to mention.

While certain regions have their particular sporting emphases—just witness the American devotion to the Super Bowl—there is one game that utterly dominates the globe. By pretty much any measure, the number one sport in the world is football (soccer). Looking at this one game alone can give us a feel for the global impact of sport. More people play football than any other sport—in 2006, 265 million people were registered in clubs or leagues.[2] If we were to include everyone who kicks a ball in their backyard, on the street or in the local park, the number would be far, far higher. And more people watch football than any other sport.[3] According to FIFA, 1.12 billion

---

[2] 'Top 10 most popular sports in the world by participation', *Pledge Sports*, June 2017: pledgesports.org/2017/06/top-10-most-popular-sports-in-the-world-by-participation/; and 'Top 10 Most Popular Participation Sports in the World' *Realbuzz.com,* 21 April 2017: realbuzz.com/articles-interests/sports-activities/article/top-10-most-popular-participation-sports-in-the-world/.

[3] 'Top 10 Most Watched Sports', *Pledge Sports,* March 2017: pledgesports.org/2017/03/top-10-most-watched-sports/.

viewers watched the 2018 World Cup Final.[4]

Of course, not everyone thinks that the high level of worldwide attention is good. Involvement with sport, as with so many other positive areas of life, can so easily degenerate into something negative. It is not hard to find people decrying sport's excessive and sometimes harmful influence, citing, for example, its capacity to distract people from family, work and study; divert money from more productive pursuits; damage character; destroy health; dominate the cultural landscape; and contribute to the decline of religion.[5] While there is some truth in these concerns, it demonstrates in yet another way the global influence of sport.

Christianity and sport

As I said earlier, I love sport. But I love God, my family, and other people a whole lot more. Thanks to the grace of God, I became a Christian when I was about ten, and have thus spent most of my sporting life as a follower of Jesus. This has given me many years to reflect on how the Bible would have me interact with sport as a believer, and plenty of opportunities

---

4   'More than half the world watched record breaking 2018 World Cup', *FIFA.com*, 21 December 2018: fifa.com/worldcup/news/more-than-half-the-world-watched-record-breaking-2018-world-cup.

5   See, for example, Sam Duncan, 'Our obsession with sport has reached religious proportions', *The Huffington Post*, 9 December 2016: huffingtonpost.com.au/sam-duncan/our-obsession-with-sport-has-reached-religious-proportions_a_21623855/; Dominic Sandbrook, 'We've never been so obsessed with sport, but there's so much of it on TV that we've become a nation of couch potato champions', *The Daily Mail,* 26 June 2012: dailymail.co.uk/news/article-2164676/.

to apply my conclusions. I recall, as a junior high schooler, sitting in the assembly hall one day considering the question of whether I would give up cricket if God asked me to. While this would be a pretty easy question for most Christians to resolve, for me it was a big issue. I wrestled with it, and eventually concluded with some reluctance that I would.

Over the years, I have realized that sport—like most areas of human endeavour—can be a real plus or a real minus for one's Christian life and for the kingdom of God. It opens up many opportunities for the believer, but also exposes them to various dangers. On the positive side, sport enables the Christian to enjoy one's self, glorify God, meet and spend time with people, encourage believers, witness to non-believers, develop one's character, improve one's health, enjoy rest and recreation, provide entertainment, and be entertained. For some it can open up opportunities to travel, and for others it may even provide employment. All of these things have been true for me, and I am very grateful for them. God has given human beings the capacity to invent sports, and, as Paul writes in 1 Timothy 4:4, "everything God created is good, and nothing is to be rejected if it is received with thanksgiving".

But, sadly, like so many other good things in God's world, sport is marred by sin and can expose a Christian to many real dangers. There is the danger of turning sport into an idol. It can become an obsession, dominate our thinking, detrimentally affect our moods, keep us away from church and Christian fellowship, and cause us to do foolish things. Participation can bring out poor sportsmanship, anger and violence. Spending extended time with non-believing sportspeople can expose the follower of Jesus to temptations such as alcohol and drug abuse, and sexual immorality. Sport *can* hinder our spiritual growth. We probably know of, or have read about, Christian sportspeople who have fallen badly into sin. Sadly, at all levels, the courts and fields of this planet are littered with people who once appeared to live as Christians, but now no longer call Jesus 'Lord'. For some, sport seems to have played a role in their demise.

Accordingly, it comes as no surprise that, throughout history, Christians have had something of a 'hot and cold' relationship with sport. The apostle Paul seemed quite fond of sporting metaphors in his letters (e.g. 1 Cor 9:24-27; Gal 5:7), whereas the early church father Tertullian asserted that the games of his day were "idolatry" and "belong to the devil".[6]

Fast forward almost 2,000 years to the 1980s. Graham Daniels was a 21-year-old playing first team professional football with Cambridge United when he was converted to the Christian faith. Not long afterwards, a kindly old gentleman from his church took him aside and said, "You'll be giving up this soccer now to concentrate on the Lord's work, won't you?" The man clearly saw little value in the game of football. Graham was shattered.[7]

Significantly, at around the same time, another older Christian man from the same church, a professor at Cambridge University, started to meet up regularly with Graham to read

---

6 Tertullian, *On the Spectacles*, chapter IV, trans. TR Glover, Loeb Classical Library 250, HUP, Cambridge, MA, 1966, p. 243.
7 Unless otherwise indicated, all direct quotations throughout this book are from personal interviews conducted by the author.

the Bible and pray. He encouraged Graham to keep playing football, which he did. These days, Graham is General Director of Christians in Sport in the UK.

So, you are a Christian and you like sport. You may be a professional sportsperson, someone for whom it is a serious part-time pursuit, or perhaps—like most people—someone who simply dabbles for a little diversion. You may be the parent of a sportsperson, a coach, a pastor, or a fan. You want to think about how Christianity and your sports involvement fit together. You know that as a follower of Jesus you are supposed to seek first God's kingdom (Matt 6:33), and to love God and your neighbour (Mark 12:28-31). How does your athletic interest fit in with this? How do they come together, rather than being two apparently separate aspects of your existence?

Thankfully, an increasing amount of academic work is being done in the area of sport and Christianity, much of which is very helpful and stimulating.[8] In addition, biographies of believing sportspeople can be found on the shelves of Christian bookstores, many of which are quite inspiring.[9] This book is a little different. It is not an academic book (although it does draw upon scholarly research), nor is it a Christian biography (although it does contain the stories and testimo-

---

[8] For a good summary, see Nick J Watson and Andrew Parker, 'Sports and Christianity: Mapping the Field', in *Sports and Christianity: Historical and Contemporary Perspectives*, Nick J Watson and Andrew Parker (eds), Routledge, New York, 2013, pp. 9-88.

[9] For example, Duncan Hamilton, *For the Glory: Olympic Legend Eric Liddell's Journey of Faith and Survival*, Penguin, New York, 2016; and Norman Grubb, *C.T. Studd: Cricketer and Pioneer*, Lutterworth, Guildford, 1982.

nies of Christian sportspeople). Rather, by drawing on the Scriptures, the writings of other Christians, my own experiences, and the experiences of other Christian sportspeople of all levels from around the world, it seeks to help the Christian person—whether player, parent or pastor—to think about sport in a Christian way.

Sport, like so many other areas of life, can be a real force for good or for evil. My hope is that this book would help us to make it the former not the latter, a plus rather than a minus for our spiritual lives, and a help rather than a hindrance to the kingdom of God.

PLAYING BY THE BOOK

What the Bible says about sport

> The LORD God took the man
> and put him in the Garden of Eden
> to work it and take care of it.
> (Genesis 2:15)

///

"Why do you play sport?" If you'd asked me that question when I was in primary school, I would have said it was because I loved it. It was fun. Arriving home from school, I didn't need much convincing to go out into the backyard and play any one of a number of games. If you'd asked me in high school why I played, I might have come up with a few more reasons. I would still have said that I played for fun; I may or may not have admitted that sporting success was good for my self-esteem; and, as a Christian, I would have been alert to the opportunities sport gave me to speak about my faith. But, if the truth be known, I was not overly reflective at the time about *why* I played sport—really, the dominant reason was because I enjoyed it.

As such, an end-of-season speech given by the coach of

the local under-16 soccer team in which I played absolutely floored me. I was stunned. Even today, over 35 years later, I still muse over his words.

Under our coach's guidance, we'd gone from being a solid suburban team to winning our local first division competition. And, in the season just completed, we had made the semi-finals of the Champion of Champions tournament—a knockout competition involving the first division premiers from around the state.

Our coach was the absolute salt of the earth. An engineer turned barrister, he had given up his Friday nights and Saturdays for about five years to look after us. We were a pretty decent bunch, but, like most teenagers, we had our moments. Our coach (almost) always bore it all in good humour as he patiently sought to teach us the basic and finer points of the game. I really liked him—as I'm pretty sure the whole team did—and I appreciated his dedication to us and to the sport. So it was with feelings of great positivity that we, players and parents alike, settled back to listen to what he had to say about the season.

I hadn't really given it much thought but, if asked, would have assumed he was going to express his appreciation to the parents and to our club. Perhaps he'd reflect on our season's success and highlight a few amusing incidents—at least that's what I would have done.

And then he said it. They may even have been his opening words: "The reason I really enjoy coaching these boys is because playing soccer is great preparation for life."

What?!?! What did he say?!?! I didn't hear anything much

after that. My mind was agog. Is *that* what he thought all this was about? I thought we were all playing (and coaching) because we liked soccer—that it was fun, a great game. I could probably even have conceded that it was good for building friendships and fitness. But I hadn't realized that it was supposed to have anything to do with 'life'.

It raises a good question: why *do* people play sport?

Why play sport?

Robert Ellis, an Oxford University academic, has addressed this very question. He undertook a survey of sportspeople in which around 100 respondents gave their reasons for participation in sport. Ellis then grouped their answers into five main categories: fitness and health; relief of general stress; social motives; enjoyment of competition; and simple enjoyment.[1] This is a good list, and one to which most sportspeople can easily relate.

But these are the sorts of reasons that people willingly shared. There are also other reasons for involvement in sport which participants may choose not to admit, or of which they may not even be aware. For example, some may play sport because of self-esteem issues or personal identity issues, to win the respect of a parent, or because they are subject to broader social forces.[2]

1 Robert Ellis, *The Games People Play: Theology, Religion, and Sport*, Wipf & Stock, Eugene, 2014, p. 168.
2 Ellis suggests some less conscious reasons for playing sport which relate to issues such as developmental needs, identity, and religious motivations (Ellis, pp. 175-89).

All these reasons, both conscious and subconscious, must be extremely powerful, given the level at which sport saturates the vast majority of cultures on the planet. But are they *good* reasons for Christians to play sport? Believers, after all, are supposed to take their cues not from what everyone else is doing, but from God and his word.

As noted earlier, and as we will see in the next chapter, Christians over the years have come to quite a range of views regarding the merits and appropriateness of believers involving themselves with sport. Some of these perspectives were well presented in the classic movie *Chariots of Fire*. This movie follows the real-life fortunes of two British runners preparing for the 1924 Paris Olympic Games—Scot Eric Liddell and Englishman Harold Abrahams.

Liddell was a committed Christian, the son of missionary parents. Fairly early in the movie and well before the Paris Olympics, Eric, his father, and another man discuss Eric's running. His father tells him, "You're the proud possessor of many gifts, and it's your sacred duty to put them to good use". The other man then notes that the Christian mission cannot but gain by Eric's athletic success: "What we need now is a muscular Christian to make folks sit up and notice."

But the film depicts Eric's sister Jennie as being not nearly as enthusiastic. She reproaches him on one occasion when he is late for a church meeting because of his running: "Training, training, training. All I ever hear is training. Do you believe in what we're doing here or not?" She later confesses, "I'm frightened for you. I'm frightened for what it all might do to you."³ Eric then tries to reassure his sister: "I believe that God made me for a purpose—for China [where he would eventually be a missionary]. But he also made me fast, and when I run, I feel his pleasure. To give it up would be to hold him in contempt."

So there we have some reasons for Christians playing sport—using one's gifts, to support Christian mission, and for the spiritual pleasure of it. We also have some reasons not to do so—the danger of exposure to bad influences, and the danger of prioritizing sport above what are perceived to be more spiritual issues.

This range of views can still be seen today. Clearly, many Christians think that involvement in sport is a positive thing. Consider the many Christian sporting organizations around the globe—for example, large international and national groups such as Christians in Sport and Athletes in Action, along with the more specialized local organizations like the South Manchester and Cheshire Christian Football League. People in these groups obviously believe there is a lot to be gained by the Christian person playing sport. I don't know of any Christian organizations that exist to *discourage* believers

---

3   While broadly accurate, the movie does take some cinematic licence. Jennie Liddell was, in fact, a young girl living with her missionary parents in China when Eric ran in Paris. See 'Jennie Liddell Biography', *IMDB:* imdb.com/name/nm0509171/bio. In real life, she was supportive of her brother's running. See Alex von Tunzelmann, 'Chariots of fire: history gets the runaround', *The Guardian*, 19 July 2012: theguardian.com/film/2012/jul/19/chariots-fire-reel-history. Nevertheless, her character in the movie exemplifies the way some Christians at the time felt about sport.

from playing sport, but anecdotal evidence of believers with more negative views are common. Consider the testimony of Graham Daniels in the introduction, who was encouraged to give up playing football soon after his conversion.

So, how *should* Christians think about sport? Is it a good thing, a bad thing, or a neutral thing? To find the answers, we need to go to God's word.

The Bible on sport

There are quite a number of references to sport in the Scriptures. And I'm not going to catalogue all those lame jokes about sport in the Bible, which involve things like 'Rebekah walking to the well with a pitcher', or 'Peter standing up with the eleven'. No, there are passages which actually do refer to sport. There are verses that speak about running a race (Ps 19:5; Gal 2:2, 5:7; Phil 2:16; 2 Tim 4:7; Heb 12:1), training (1 Tim 4:8), and winning a prize (Phil 3:14; 2 Tim 2:5, 4:8). One passage talks about all three, plus boxing:

> Do you not know that in a race all the runners run, but only one gets the prize? Run in such a way as to get the prize. Everyone who competes in the games goes into strict training. They do it to get a crown that will not last, but we do it to get a crown that will last forever. Therefore I do not run like someone running aimlessly; I do not fight like a boxer beating the air. No, I strike a blow to my body and make it my slave so that after I have preached to others, I myself will not be disqualified for the prize. (1 Cor 9:24-27)

While highly evocative, these passages are really using sport to help illustrate other points—for example, living the Christian life, godliness, perseverance and hope. They are not primarily seeking to teach us about sport—for example, *whether, why, how,* and *how much* we should play sport. To think about these sorts of questions, we will need to take more general biblical teaching and apply it to the topic of sport. Thankfully, there has been an increasing amount of thought given to this area over recent decades.[4]

Since we are going to apply biblical principles to sport, it would be helpful at this point to set out what exactly we mean by *sport* and also by the related nouns *play* and *game*. *Play* might be defined as an unstructured activity undertaken for its own sake—to creatively enjoy something for its own intrinsic good. An example would be throwing a rock at a can placed on a wall. A *game* is play where rules are added, such as a game of chasings played in a school playground. Finally, *sport* is where the rules of a game are universalized and a sense of genuine competition is added. It usually involves physical and mental exertion, and is marked by a significant element of skill that can be refined by practice. Examples of sport would be football, basketball and cricket.[5] Thus, *sport* can be understood as a subset of *games*, which is a subset of *play*.

---

[4] See Jeremy R Treat, 'More than a Game: A Theology of Sport', *Themelios*, vol. 40, no. 3, December 2015, p. 392; and Watson and Parker, pp. 9-88. For the structure of this chapter—particularly definitions, and the concepts of delighting in and developing creation, the intrinsic and instrumental value of sport, and the dangers of idolatry and immorality—I was greatly assisted by Treat's article.

[5] For these definitions see Ellis, pp. 3, 128-9; and Treat, pp. 395-6.

We can find the theological basis for play, games and sport in the creation account. Genesis 1:31 tells us, "God saw all that he had made, and it was very good". God places humanity into this beautiful creation and gives them the opportunity to freely enjoy almost all of it: "And the LORD God commanded the man, 'You are free to eat from any tree in the garden; but you must not eat from the tree of the knowledge of good and evil'" (Gen 2:16-17). Of course, we know the man ended up eating from the tree from which he was forbidden to eat, but this should not blind us to the fact that everything else there was open to humanity for their enjoyment and delight. Except for the tree of knowledge of good and evil, *all* of God's creation was there for humanity to appreciate.

Sport, of course, is not a naturally occurring phenomenon. But humanity was not intended to simply *delight* in the creation—we were also called to *develop* it. God told humanity in Genesis 1:28 to "fill the earth and subdue it", and then Genesis 2:15 says: "The LORD God took the man and put him in the Garden of Eden to work it and take care of it". The instruction to subdue the earth and take care of the garden—that is, to develop creation—is essentially a command to create culture. This is sometimes referred to as the *cultural mandate*.[6] As John Stott has said: "'Nature' is what God gives; 'culture' is what we

---

[6] On the cultural mandate, see Michael W Goheen and Craig G Bartholomew, *Living at the Crossroads: An Introduction to Christian Worldview*, Baker, Grand Rapids, 2008, pp. 153-4; and Treat, pp. 394-5. The term 'cultural mandate' can be associated with a variety of views around Christian involvement in culture and politics. I am simply using the term here to describe developing creation or creating culture as per Genesis 1:28 and 2:15.

do with it".[7] Sport, along with numerous other activities such as music, dance and literature, is just one of the ways in which culture has been developed. It has been reasonably asserted that the God-given instinct to play "would inevitably develop into something more".[8]

It is also intriguing to note that play does not appear to be simply a temporal concern. Play, it seems, will be found in the new creation:

> This is what the LORD Almighty says: "Once again men and women of ripe old age will sit in the streets of Jerusalem, each of them with cane in hand because of their age. The city streets will be filled with boys and girls playing there." (Zech 8:4-5)

Sport has *intrinsic* value

So it can be said that sport (a subset of play) has *intrinsic* value—that is, it is good in and of itself. God has created us and placed us in a good world, and he has given us the cultural mandate along with the ingenuity to fulfil that mandate. Sport is one of the good things that has arisen as a result. Unless their rules are unethical—for example, fight-to-the-death gladiatorial contests—sports can be viewed as gifts from God to be enjoyed with thanksgiving (1 Tim 4:4).

Having made the point that sport has intrinsic value, let's

---

7   John W Stott, *New Issues Facing Christians Today*, 3rd edn, Marshall Pickering, London, 1999, p. 193.
8   Treat, p. 395.

address a few potential concerns—unhelpful dualistic views, and doubts about the very idea of competition.

Dualistic views

Some people may disagree with the assertion that sport is an intrinsically good gift from God if they are affected by either of two unhelpful forms of dualistic thinking—"an ascetic body/soul dualism" that sees sport as bad, or "a sacred/secular dualism" that views sport as merely neutral.[9]

An unbiblical body/soul dualism has sometimes been imported into Christian thinking. The early church developed in a world that was strongly influenced by Greek thought—a strong strand of which elevated the soul and the spiritual, and downplayed the body and the physical. Some of this thinking wrongly crept into Christian belief. By contrast, the Scriptures teach that God created the physical world, including our bodies, and pronounced it "good" (Gen 1:31). How could something that God created and pronounced 'good' be bad or of little importance? We must not let Greek-style dualistic thinking negatively influence our thinking about the body, about the physical, and about sport.[10]

But another unhelpful distinction can also affect our thinking here: sacred/secular dualism. According to this view, God cares about *sacred* activities such as prayer, Bible study, evangelism and church, while *secular* activities such as work, sport,

---

9   Treat, p. 397.
10 On this form of dualistic thinking, see Treat, p. 397; and Watson and Parker, p. 17.

music and art are neutral and only matter to God if they are promoting some sacred activity. The fact that sacred activities are clearly of immense importance should not lead us to conclude that other activities that involve developing and delighting in God's creation, such as sport, are merely neutral. No, sport is intrinsically good.

Competition

Another area of concern for some is competition. Theologians Michael W Goheen and Craig G Bartholomew suggest that "sports and competition [...] are gifts of God in creation, to be richly enjoyed with thanksgiving".[11] Wait a second! Can we say that *competition* is a gift from God? Doesn't competition lead to a whole lot of unhealthy and negative consequences such as abuse, cheating, hatred and violence? What about that quote from the legendary American football coach Vince Lombardi: "To play [football] you must have fire in you, and there is nothing that stokes that fire like hate"?[12]

Of course—as with every other form of human culture—competitive sport, when impacted by sin, produces very negative results, and we will discuss sin's impact on sport throughout this book. But competition in itself is not a bad thing. It can be a very good thing that enhances the athletic experience and, in some cases, is almost essential to the athletic experience. Goheen and Bartholomew argue, "In sports, teams or individuals agree cooperatively to oppose one another within the

---

11 Goheen and Bartholomew, p. 153.
12 Goheen and Bartholomew, p. 154.

eg both agree to compete

stated goals, rules, and obstacles of the game. In other words, cooperation, not rivalry, is at the heart of competition." If you want a good game of basketball, you need a team to play against. We can love our neighbour by providing stiff competition.[13] I can certainly testify that some of my most satisfying sporting experiences have been close games or athletic competitions—some of which I won, and some of which I lost.

Sport has *instrumental* value

So, we have argued that sport has *intrinsic* value. But sport also has immense *instrumental* value—that is, participation in it can lead to many other positive outcomes.

We do not have to look far to find people singing the praises of the instrumental benefits of sport. The Western Australian Government's Department of Local Government, Sport and Cultural Industries lists 30 ways in which sport and recreation benefits people and communities.[14] Some of these benefits include:

» bringing people together, providing opportunities for social interaction
» contributing to higher levels of self-esteem and self-worth

---

13 On the potentially positive aspects of competition, including the quote, see Goheen and Bartholomew, p. 154.
14 'Sport and recreation research and policy', *Government of Western Australia,* 3 July 2019: dlgsc.wa.gov.au/sport-and-recreation/benefits-to-the-community.

- » creating positive alternatives to youth offending, anti-social behaviour, and crime
- » healthy workers are more productive and take fewer sick days
- » improvements in mental health.

Sport is very often seen as promoting character and physical health. American tennis great Billie Jean King has said that sport "teaches you character, it teaches you to play by the rules, it teaches you to know what it feels like to win and lose—it teaches you about life".[15] It was this sort of benefit that was spoken of by my under-16s soccer coach all those years ago. Indian cricket superstar Kapil Dev affirmed sport's physical benefits when he said, "Apart from education, you need good health, and for that, you need to play sports".[16]

As Christians, we will add our own instrumental benefits to the list set out above. We would want to add, for example, that sport can provide ways to promote evangelism, and provide opportunities to encourage other believers. We'll say much more about these benefits in chapters to come.

---

15 'Trailblazer and Changemaker: Billie Jean King', *National Coalition of Girls' Schools*, 22 February 2018: ncgs.org/advocacy/blog/2018/02/22/trailblazer-and-changemaker-billie-jean-king/.
16 'Education and Good Health are Essence of Life and Sports Boost them Further', *Be an Inspirer*, 20 June 2019: beaninspirer.com/education-and-good-health-are-essence-of-life-and-sports-boost-them-further/.

The impact of sin on sport

So, sport is a good gift of God. But, as I expect is painfully clear to most of us, sport, like all areas of life, is impacted by sin. And sin is insidious. It can take a good thing like sport and twist it into, or associate it with, something bad—*immorality*; it can also take a good thing and seek to elevate it into an ultimate thing—*idolatry*.[17] While we will consider the dangers associated with sport in the chapters that follow, it might be helpful to expand briefly on idolatry and immorality here.

Idolatry

Idolatry takes something and puts it in the place of God. It is the idol rather than God that determines how we live. It is not hard to find apparent examples in the world of sport. For example, Bill Shankly, the legendary Liverpool Football Club manager from 1959 to 1974, is alleged to have said: "Some people believe football is a matter of life and death, I am very disappointed with that attitude. I can assure you it is much, much more important than that."[18]

Articles describing the idolatrous influence of sport (although they don't usually use that term) are similarly easy to locate. Consider the following extracts from three different countries:

---

17 Treat, p. 398. Actually, idolatry can be understood as taking anything—good or bad—and putting it in the place of God in one's life.
18 Ellis, p. 165.

> As a nation, Australia's obsession with sport has reached religious proportions. We are more religious about sport than religion itself.[19]

> For we [the writer is in the UK] live in an era when, thanks to television, sport is marketed as a matter of life and death.[20]

> These days, it seems as if America's No. 1 priority isn't peace, equality, justice, or caring for our fellow Americans—it's sports.[21]

Resisting the idolatrous allure of sport may take some work. Robert Ellis has suggested that sport has, for some, "taken on some of the characteristics of religion, and that it may exercise functions in the individual, social, and cultural lives similar to the functions that were once exercised by organized religion". He notes that sport, like organized religion, has ritualistic, mythological, doctrinal, ethical, social, experiential, and material dimensions.[22] It comes as no surprise that, for many, sport becomes a god.

Strictly speaking, Christians cannot be guilty of idolatry as Christians cannot have something other than God occupying God's place in their lives. However, Christians can experience

---

19 Duncan, 'Our Obsession With Sport Has Reached Religious Proportions'.
20 Sandbrook, 'We've never been so obsessed with sport, but there's so much of it on TV that we've become a nation of couch potato champions'.
21 Frank Carson, '10 Reasons Sports are America's No. 1 Priority', *The Cheat Sheet*, 8 January 2015: cheatsheet.com/sports/10-reasons-sports-are-americas-no-1-priority.html.
22 Ellis, pp. 108-22; cf. Treat, p. 399.

the tempting allure of sporting idolatry, and for some there may be a real danger of adopting what we might call an *idolatrous attitude* towards sport—that is, developing an unhelpful obsession with, or reliance on, sport. For example, for some believers sport is not so much an idol as a crutch. We become a little too reliant on it. We are Christians; God is first in our lives; we find our significance, identity and self-worth in him—mostly. But perhaps, without our realizing it, sport is something that helps prop up our self-image. We don't just enjoy sport; we start to lean on it. But only God can bear the weight of providing our ultimate sense of self-worth and happiness.

Immorality

Sport's association with various forms of immorality is also a real problem. In their overview of research on the ethics of sport, Watson and Parker set out some of the key danger areas:

- » physical and verbal abuse of opponents (and even teammates)
- » fan violence, including sectarianism
- » intimidation and trash talk
- » cheating, and blatant disregard for the spirit of the rules
- » mistaking legality for ethicality
- » sexual abuse of athletes by coaches
- » trash talk
- » financial greed and corruption
- » alienation in individual and international relations
- » invasive noncorrective surgery to enhance athletic performance

» drug-doping
» abuse of officials
» genetic-enhancement technologies
» abusive child and youth elite development academies
» overtraining and abuse of one's body
» the potential deleterious effects of excessive expectation and pressure from parents, coaches, and even nations.[23]

Wow! The list takes some digesting, and the sad thing is that we could all probably add a few further items. I can recall a few occasions where I failed in a couple of the listed areas, and I've also witnessed other Christian sportspeople similarly struggle at times.

Sport can also be associated with immorality off the field as well as on it. In my experience, and from speaking with many other Christian sportsmen and women of all standards around the world, the most widespread off-field dangers are excessive alcohol consumption and sexual immorality—perils found in many other spheres of life. Sadly, there are many examples of Christians involved in top-flight sport who have fallen badly and publicly when faced with temptations in these areas.

Living as a Christian in a sporting context—or any context, for that matter—involves struggle. The stronger our relationship with God, the better we will do. But none of us are perfect.

Former Australian rugby union captain Nick Farr-Jones became a Christian in his teenage years. He has sought to live out his faith both during and after his international career

---

23 Watson and Parker, pp. 28-9.

in a variety of positive ways. Reflecting honestly on his playing days, he admits that he sometimes found the context of international sport very challenging for his Christian faith. "I stumbled from time to time," he confesses, "but that is the great thing about the cross—we are forgiven for all the times we have fallen short". That is a hugely encouraging truth!

Perspective and priority

So there are many good reasons to play sport (both intrinsic and instrumental) and there are many dangers to avoid (idolatrous attitudes and immorality). But as potentially great as it can be, for the Christian sport is not the main game—following Jesus is. God has shown his incredible love for us in many ways—particularly in sending his Son for us (John 3:16). Our priority is to seek first the kingdom of God and his righteousness (Matt 6:33). In doing this, we strive to love God and our neighbours in ways that are consistent with Scripture (e.g. Mark 12:28-31; John 14:15; Rom 13:8), knowing that God's Spirit motivates and empowers us for this task (Phil 2:13). Some athletes prioritize their sport and fit the rest of their lives around it; Christians prioritize God and fit all aspects of their life—including sport—around serving him. Many athletes hope for medals, trophies and premierships. Those can be good things. But Christians also seek something far greater:

> Everyone who competes in the games goes into strict training. They do it to get a crown that will not last, but we do it to get a crown that will last forever. (1 Cor 9:25)

How much better to have God say to us "Well done, good and faithful servant!" (Matt 25:21) at the end of our lives than to have a sporting official hang a medal around our neck.

Living a life devoted to serving God will see us want to live in a close relationship with God. We'll also want to help others to get into and live in a close relationship with God. This will mean prioritizing Bible reading, prayer, fellowship, discipleship, evangelism, serving others, family relationships, and using our gifts in ways appropriate to our life circumstances. How this will impact someone's sport will vary from person to person. For some, wise Christian living may mean playing a lot of sport; for others, it will mean a moderate amount of sport; and for yet others it will mean no sport at all.

It is interesting to contrast two Christians who were also English cricketing greats. One, CT Studd, a popular test cricketer of the 1880s, stopped playing competitive sport soon after his conversion. Another, David Sheppard, an international of the 1950s and 60s, played cricket and represented his country for a number of years after his ordination as an Anglican minister.[24]

Some people reading this book may be nervous about putting their sporting life under the lordship of Christ. A voice in the back of their heads may tell them that God is a killjoy and wants to rip them off. It may whisper that perhaps it's okay to give some areas of their life to God, but not their sport. Could I just say that we can trust all aspects of our lives—including our sporting involvement—to God.

---

24 Ellis, p. 85.

"For God so loved the world that he gave his one and only Son, that whoever believes in him shall not perish but have eternal life." (John 3:16)

We can trust everything to someone who loves us that much. Furthermore, I would argue that we get more out of our sporting lives by putting God first. I believe I enjoyed my sport a lot more over the years by doing this.

Men's tennis was massive in the 1980s with greats like Bjorn Borg, John McEnroe and Jimmy Connors dominating the world stage. During that time, an American Christian by the name of Gene Mayer rose to become the fourth best player in the world. He was extremely talented, but for Gene, tennis was not his life—it was part of his Christian life. He once said, "I acknowledged before God that my tennis was his". This shaped the way he arranged his life. Could he have made number one in the world? Gene explains:

> In order to have possibly been number one in the world, it would have taken a rearrangement of my priorities, which I [was] not willing to do. [...My priorities were] first, having a relationship with God that is healthy, then, having a healthy relationship with my family, and then to think of tennis as my occupation.[25]

As wonderful as sport can be, there is something far better.

---

25 Andrew Wingfield Digby, *The Loud Appeal: Playing by God's Rules*, Hodder & Stoughton, London, 1988, pp. 110-11.

PAST AND PRESENT
The history of Christianity and sport[1]

> **Follow my example,**
> **as I follow the example of Christ.**
> **(1 Corinthians 11:1)**

///

Two-time Olympic rowing silver-medallist Debbie Flood came to the sport which brought her to international prominence later than most. Growing up in Yorkshire with active parents, athletic endeavour and outdoor activities were always high on the agenda. The family did lots of running, walking and cycling together, and Debbie's parents also encouraged her and her brother in their sports. A Christian from her teenage years, Debbie revelled in this sort of physical activity and

---

1   Much of the information in this chapter comes from four very helpful works: William J Baker, *Playing with God: Religion and Modern Sport,* HUP, Cambridge, MA, 2007; Ellis, *The Games People Play*; Tony Ladd and James A Mathisen, *Muscular Christianity: Evangelical Protestants and the Development of American Sport*, Baker, Grand Rapids, 1999; and Watson and Parker (eds), *Sports and Christianity*.

eventually became a Great Britain junior judo representative, and competed at county level in cross-country running, the 1500 metres, and shot put.

Her move to rowing was quite unplanned. An elderly gentleman spotted her working out on a rowing machine at a local gym. He noticed that her performance on this piece of equipment was exceptionally good, and suggested that she try some actual rowing. Debbie decided to give it a go and soon joined Bradford Rowing Club. Her rise was meteoric. Within a few years, she was rowing for Great Britain in the women's quadruple sculls at the 2004 Athens Olympic Games, winning silver. She repeated this feat at Beijing in 2008.

Having not grown up with rowing, Debbie has over the years done some reading on the history of the sport—particularly women's rowing. "It is fascinating," she says, "and has given me a deeper respect for the sport". Women's rowing only became part of the Olympic program in 1976. "I am very respectful of those pioneering women who led the way in women's rowing", Debbie says. "I appreciate where we are today, and know that we are standing today on the shoulders of those who went before us."

We can learn from the past in all areas of human activity. History can tell us how we got to where we are today, and where we might go in the future. Accordingly, we can gain a lot of insight into contemporary issues concerning Christianity and sport by knowing a little bit about the history of their relationship.

The short historical summary that follows will give us some context within which to place whatever knowledge we possess on this topic. And, just as the Bible urges us to learn from both good examples (1 Cor 11:1) and bad examples (1 Cor 10:6) in biblical history, so too we can learn from the good and bad examples that make up the history of Christianity and sport.

Games, gods and gore: Games and religion in the ancient world

The relationship between games and religion is not new—it goes back at least a few thousand years.[2] There is evidence of an ancient Central American ball game being played from about 1500 BC up until around 1500 AD. While there seems to have been a few versions, it essentially involved two teams on a court trying to get a ball through an elevated hoop in something of a cross between football, lacrosse, basketball and volleyball. While the game could be played for entertainment, it often seems to have been a more serious affair with religious symbolism and at times grisly results. Sometimes at the game's end—and there is some debate over what exactly took place at this point—the winning captain may have executed the losing captain, or perhaps had his own head cut off, thus earning

---

2   Ellis argues that sport as we currently think of it, with its more "universalized and bureaucratized forms", could be understood as being less than 200 years old. That said, he does recognize that many of the organized games of the ancient world had, to varying degrees, attributes in common with modern-day sport. For convenience, however, I will usually refer to all 'sport-like' activities that take place before 1800 as *games*, and the activities that started to develop from that time on as *sports*. See Ellis, pp. 3-4.

him an immediate trip to paradise.³ Sport in ancient Central America really could be a matter of life and death!

Over in Greece, things were a little more civilized. The ancient Olympic Games, held in honour of the Greek god Zeus, traditionally date from 776 BC and took place at Olympus. Other ancient games were also subsequently held at places like Delphi (in honour of Apollo), Corinth (in honour of Poseidon), Nemea (in honour of Zeus), and Athens (in honour of Athena). There were also numerous other smaller-scale religious athletic festivals. Athletes would gather from different regions and compete in events such as horse racing, chariot racing, foot racing, boxing, wrestling, and the pentathlon (which involved running, long jump, discus, javelin and wrestling). These events were interwoven with religious ceremonies such as oaths, animal sacrifices and processions. As is the case today, stadia needed to be built, athletes received financial reward and public acclaim, gambling took place, and scandals, bribery and cheating were commonplace.⁴

As the Roman Empire rose to prominence in the century before Christ, the Romans developed their own more brutal spin on public athletic events. They staged highly dangerous chariot races and gladiatorial contests involving man versus man, man versus animal, and animal versus animal. A glad-

---

3 On the ancient Central American ball game, see Baker, pp. 6-7; and Ellis, pp. 4-5.
4 On the Greek games, see Baker, pp. 9-10; Ellis, pp. 6-8; Everett Ferguson, *Backgrounds of Early Christianity*, 3rd edn, Eerdmans, Grand Rapids, 2003, pp. 100-1; and Shirl James Hoffman, *Good Game: Christianity and the Culture of Sports*, Baylor University Press, Waco, 2010, pp. 26-7.

iator was a combination of skilled athlete and trained killer. As jobs go, it was not a long-term proposition, with most eventually dying in the arena. Again stadia needed to be built, prizemoney was offered, and gambling took place. Crowd behaviour could be fanatical and violent. The Roman games also had religious overtones, with gladiators swearing sacred oaths. It has been said that these Roman spectacles also served as a way of keeping the masses amused, preventing them from becoming bored or dissatisfied with the regime: "Life was cheap in Roman sport."[5]

Running the race? Games and Christianity in the early church

While the Greek games were still taking place during New Testament times, the Roman spectacles had really come into prominence. So how were games viewed by the writers of the Bible? As noted in the previous chapter, there are verses that refer to running a race (Ps 19:5; 1 Cor 9:24-26; Gal 2:2, 5:7; Phil 2:16; 2 Tim 4:7; Heb 12:1), to boxing (1 Cor 9:26), to training (1 Cor 9:25; 1 Tim 4:8), and to winning a prize (1 Cor 9:25; Phil 3:14; 2 Tim 2:5; 4:8). The apostle Paul wrote most of these passages. With their references to running and boxing, the majority appear to refer more to the Greek expression of games than to the Roman versions.

Does Paul's use of such language in the Scriptures indicate

---

5 Ellis, p. 10-11 (quote from p. 10); cf. Baker, p. 11; Ferguson, pp. 102-3; Hoffman, pp. 29-35.

his approval of Greek games? Not necessarily, given that athletic metaphorical language seems to have been "part of the stock-in-trade of popular philosophers and moralists" of the day.[6] That said, it is unlikely that Paul would have used something that was inherently evil as a metaphor for the Christian life. For example, can you imagine him describing the spiritual focus of the Christian life in the following terms: "Just as every assassin undertakes strict preparation so that they will succeed in their task, prepare in such a way that you will terminate your target and gain your reward"? No, Paul's use of athletic metaphors suggests he either views those aspects of the Greek games that did not conflict with Christian morality neutrally or with some level of positivity. Given that elsewhere he writes that "physical training is of some value" (1 Tim 4:8), is seems likely that he has some level of approval towards such games.

If Paul possessed some level of positivity towards the ethical aspects of Greek games, the same cannot be said of early Christian attitudes towards the Roman games. As noted, these spectacles were high on violence and death, and were associated with gambling, poor crowd behaviour, and pagan religions. Christians could be killed in the arena.[7] Early in the second century, the bishop and martyr Ignatius described the violence that took place in the Roman amphitheatre as "cruel

---

6   Ferguson, pp. 101-2.
7   Ivor J Davidson, *The Birth of the Church: From Jesus to Constantine, AD 30-312*, Monarch, Oxford, 2005, pp. 189-212.

tortures inflicted by the devil".[8] In the fourth century, Theodore of Mopsuestia warns baptismal candidates to shun "the circus, the racecourse, the contest of athletes [...] which the Devil introduced into the world under the pretext of amusement, and through which he leads the souls of men to perdition".[9] Some of these warnings not only highlight the potential harm of such games, but also suggest that numbers of Christians were attending, or were tempted to attend, these events.

Harmless recreation? Games and Christianity from the fifth to 18th century

In Europe between the fifth and 15th centuries, things settled down somewhat, with different sorts of games coming to the fore. These were less bloodthirsty and seemed to have been more for the participant than the spectator. While our knowledge is sketchy, there seems to have been activities resembling bowling, football, shinty, and hurling, along with combat of various sorts, archery, racing, and recreation involving animals.[10] Games were often associated with the church. Easter celebrations, for example, often involved various forms of ball play.

---

8 Ignatius, *To the Romans*, 5:3, in *Epistles of St. Clement of Rome and St. Ignatius of Antioch*, trans. James A Kleist, Ancient Christian Writers 1, Newman Press, New York, 1946, p. 82.
9 W Laistner, *Christian and Pagan Culture in the Later Roman Empire*, Cornell University Press, Ithaca, 1951, p. 42; cited in Shirl James Hoffman, 'Harvesting Souls in the Stadium: The Rise of Sports Evangelism', in Watson and Parker (eds), *Sport and Christianity*, p. 131.
10 The games involving animals could, of course, be bloodthirsty for the animals.

Besides incorporating certain games into the religious program, the church helped popularize such forms of play by providing the time and, sometimes, the space for recreation. People worked for six days, but the seventh was a day of rest. After Sunday morning church, the afternoon could be used for games. And, if there was no village green or common area available, these recreations might take place in church grounds.

Clerical support for such pursuits, however, was not always unreserved. Some were concerned about the roughness of certain games, the property damage they could cause, and the gambling that was sometimes associated with them. Peasant football, for example, had few rules, no team size and no physical boundaries, and might be played by those who'd had too much to drink. It isn't too hard to imagine things getting out of hand. Church concerns tended to be not so much with the games themselves, but rather with what was often associated with them.[11]

When the Renaissance commenced around the 14th century it involved, among other things, the rediscovery of the classical culture of ancient Greece. This "brought a new appreciation of the aesthetics of the human body, including a positive evaluation of athletic exercise".[12] The Dutch priest and humanist Desiderius Erasmus, for example, considered tennis a perfect game for exercising all parts of the body.[13]

The Reformation of the 16th century saw games attract a somewhat mixed reaction from the movement's leaders.

11 On games in the Middle Ages, see Baker, pp. 13-15; Ellis, pp. 14-17.
12 Ellis, p. 17.
13 Baker, p. 15.

Martin Luther approved of honourable and useful games such as archery, fencing, gymnastics and wrestling. Personally, he took part in an old version of bowling. A little more cautious, John Calvin participated in bowling and quoits, but was critical of many other games, particularly when they were associated with gambling, drunkenness and misuse of the Sabbath.

The English Puritans of the 16th and 17th centuries were perhaps more pronounced in their disapproval of games, although again their objections were often not so much with the games themselves as with the behaviour often associated with them, and with their being played on Sundays. King James issued his *Declaration on Lawful Sports* in 1617. This stated that once Sunday morning church services had finished, people should be able to enjoy "harmless recreation" such as dancing, archery, leaping, and vaulting. This was a little too lenient for the Puritans.[14]

Muscular Christianity? Sport and Christianity in the 19th century

Things become far more familiar as we reach the 19th century. Modern sport as we know it really developed during this time as people found themselves with sufficient leisure time to enjoy it, and as key institutions in England such as the public schools and the churches gave it their support.[15] The assistance of the churches is noteworthy given the fact that, at the start

---

14 Baker, p. 15-17 (quote from p. 17); cf. Ellis, pp. 18-20; Watson and Parker, pp. 9-10.
15 On leisure time, see Ellis, p. 31.

of the century, clergy of all denominations—like the Puritans of previous centuries—were hostile to many aspects of sport.[16]

Signs of a thaw can be seen by the 1840s. On 6 August 1843, *Bell's Life in London*, an English sporting paper, wrote of a Buckinghamshire village where the youth gathered on a Sunday to "pursue the disreputable game of pitch and toss". The local vicar had formed a cricket club and presented them with a stock of bats, balls and stumps, and "those pernicious pursuits have now been discontinued". The paper called on other gentlemen to follow the clergyman's example.[17] It seems that ministers around this time were becoming increasingly open to cricket, with *Bell's* reporting on 29 June 1851 that many continued playing after their ordination. The paper pointed out that there were three clergy playing for Leicestershire and two for Nottinghamshire.[18]

In the 1850s, the bonds between Christianity and sport tightened with the birth of "muscular Christianity". This movement originally saw sport as a means for the building of character—character that displayed "fair play, respect (both for oneself and others), strength (physical and emotional), perseverance, deference, subordination, obedience, discipline, loyalty, cooperation, self-control, self-sacrifice, endurance".[19]

Perhaps the most well-known expression of the early muscu-

---

16 Hugh McLeod, 'Sport and Religion in England, c. 1790-1914', in Watson and Parker (eds), *Sport and Christianity*, p. 113.
17 McLeod, p. 114.
18 McLeod, p. 115.
19 Mike Collins and Andrew Parker, 'Faith and Sport Revival in Britain: Muscular Christianity and Beyond', *Stadion: International Journal of the History of Sport*, vol. 35, 2009, p. 194; cited in Watson and Parker, p. 20.

lar Christianity movement is the novel *Tom Brown's School Days*, written by Thomas Hughes and published in 1857. The book is set in Rugby School and "connects games with moral fibre, heroism, and manliness, and (even if tenuously) with Christian virtue".[20] Hughes was part of the Christian Socialist movement, with many of the muscular Christianity pioneers coming from the liberal or Broad Church wing of Anglicanism.[21]

However, the evangelical churches were also becoming more involved, seeing sport as an opportunity not only for character formation in individuals and communities, but also for evangelistic outreach.[22] In 1854, an evangelical minister, the Rev John Cale Miller of St Martin's, Birmingham, "founded a Working Men's Association which soon had seventeen hundred members, including three hundred women, and a program that included cricket and football, as well as excursions, lectures and Bible studies".[23] Churches helped start up sporting clubs across the country, and it is interesting to note that about a third of the clubs who have played football in the English Premier League were founded by churches, including Aston Villa and Everton (Methodist), and Tottenham Hotspur and Manchester City (Anglican).[24] The alliance between Christianity and sport became strongest in two quite different contexts—in the public schools, and in the working-class districts of the cities.[25]

---

20 Ellis, p. 29.
21 McLeod, p. 116; Watson and Parker, p. 20.
22 Ellis, pp. 32-3.
23 McLeod, p. 118.
24 Ellis, p. 32; cf. Peter Lupson, *Thank God for Football*, SPCK, London, 2006.
25 Baker, p. 31; McLeod, pp. 117-18.

In the 1880s, seven young men applied to become missionaries in China with the China Inland Mission. The group included English test cricketer CT Studd and Stanley P Smith, a rower from Cambridge University. They became known as the 'Cambridge Seven' and really caught the imagination of the British public. Prior to their departure, they toured the country speaking evangelistically and calling people to consider the missionary endeavour. After Studd and Smith spoke at a student gathering in Edinburgh, a Dr DA Moxey wrote:

> Students, like other young men, are apt to regard professedly religious men of their own age as wanting in manliness, unfit for the river or cricket field, and only good for Psalm-singing and pulling a long face, but the big, muscular hands and the long arms of the ex-captain of the Cambridge Eight, stretched out in entreaty while he eloquently told of the story of redeeming Love, capsized their theory; and when Mr CT Studd, a name to them familiar as a household word, and perhaps the greatest gentleman bowler in England, supplemented his brother athlete's words by quiet but intense and burning utterances of personal testimony of the love and power of a personal Saviour, opposition and criticism were alike disarmed.[26]

This was the first prominent example of sporting stars being used for Christian outreach.[27]

While women's sport had been of little interest to the founders of the muscular Christianity movement, by the late

---

26 Grubb, pp. 41-8 (quote from pp. 43-4).
27 McLeod, p. 126.

19th century things had changed. In the 1880s, sport had become part of the syllabus at girls' public schools, and increasing numbers of women were hunting, cycling, swimming, doing gymnastics, and playing croquet, tennis, and cricket.[28]

In the second half of the 19th century, muscular Christianity crossed the Atlantic to the United States.[29] It quickly gained traction through the work of the Young Men's Christian Association (YMCA) and the ministry of evangelist Dwight L Moody. The YMCA, which originally sought to distract young men from worldly recreations, soon developed a more holistic view of its mission. They increasingly provided gymnasiums and offered a variety of sports.[30] One YMCA sports coach, James Naismith, invented the game of basketball "in an effort to find a wholesome all-weather outlet for the energies of young men".[31] Another YMCA worker approvingly said, "These associations have wrestled the gymnasium from the hands of prize-fighters and professional athletes and put it into the hands of Christian gymnasts who are after the souls of men as well as their bodies".[32]

Moody was very much pro-sport. His promotion of muscular Christianity can be seen in the annual Northfield Conferences he held, beginning in 1886. These conferences attracted Christian college students and emphasized biblical instruction and the development of a 'consecrated life'. In the

---

28 McLeod, p. 117.
29 Baker, pp. 33-4; Hoffman, 'Harvesting Souls in the Stadium', p. 135.
30 Baker, pp. 42-64; Ellis, p. 30.
31 Ellis, p. 30.
32 Ladd and Mathisen, p. 57.

afternoons, participants engaged in organized activities such as baseball, football, tennis, boating and swimming. Moody was very keen to use sport for evangelism and discipleship.[33]

In Australia, from the very beginnings of its late 18th century European settlement, sport was very much part of life. Horse-racing and cricket, in particular, were prominent during the early days.[34] The colony grew slowly and steadily during the 19th century until the 1850s, when the gold rushes pushed it into overdrive. Not only did this decade see a dramatic increase in Australia's population; it also saw a great increase in enthusiasm for sports. Historian Geoffrey Blainey comments: "British sports such as horse-racing, football, cricket, boxing, rowing—and later golf and lawn tennis—migrated with ease to Australia".[35]

From the earliest days of the colony, sport was very heavily associated with gambling, and this was a significant problem for the churches.[36] However, attitudes eventually began to shift. In the 1860s and 70s, the middle classes were enjoying a golden age, with many adopting some of the values of British muscular Christianity. They came to believe in the value of sport for building moral character, with the Australian private schools (the equivalent of the English public schools) seeing sport as a way to "prepare boys for leadership roles in govern-

---

33 Ladd and Mathisen, pp. 51-7.
34 David Bruce Tyndall, *Evangelicalism, Sport and the Australian Olympics*, PhD thesis presented to Macquarie University for the degree of Doctor of Philosophy, 2004, pp. 51-3.
35 Geoffrey Blainey, *A Shorter History of Australia*, Vintage, Milsons Point, 2000, p. 109.
36 Tyndall, p. 57.

ment, business, the professions and family life".[37]

In many respects, by the end of the 19th century in the English-speaking world, Christianity and sport were starting to fit together nicely. There was widespread recognition that sport provided opportunities to build character and community, enjoy recreation, and promote evangelism and discipleship. However, tensions remained. Hugh McLeod identifies four major areas of concern: "the impact of professionalism, the persistence of gambling, differing ideas on the use of time (including Sunday) and the fear that sport was becoming 'a new religion'."[38] These concerns would only increase in subsequent centuries.

Modern sport: Sport and Christianity in the 20th and 21st centuries

The trends set at the end of the 19th century have continued to the present day. The opportunities sport provides have been very helpfully developed, while at the same time the dangers associated with it have only increased.[39] While many of these opportunities and dangers will be addressed in subsequent chapters, here we will highlight a few important 20th-century distinctives.

37 Douglas Booth and Colin Tatz, *One-Eyed: A View of Australian Sport*, Allen & Unwin, Sydney, 2000, pp. 48-9 (quote from p. 49).
38 McLeod, p. 122.
39 Ladd and Mathisen suggest that evangelical Christians "who had earlier embraced sport to accomplish God's redemptive purposes, now found themselves trapped by the values and structures of an institution rapidly moving in a different direction" (p. 78).

On the positive side, there has been the further development of evangelism through sport, the birth of Christian sports organizations, and the rise of sport chaplaincies. The problematic issue of whether to participate in sport on Sunday has also been debated and discussed over a long period of time. And on the negative side, there has been a lack of practical reflection on sport and Christianity, and the popularization of what has been described as *sportianity*.

Let's briefly examine each of these issues.

Some positives

While Christians have been using sport to assist evangelism since the mid-19th century, this ministry developed significantly during the 20th century. The great evangelist Billy Graham was one to make use of the opportunities. On one occasion in 1947, when Graham was speaking at an evangelistic meeting in North Carolina, a local Christian runner named Gil Dodds—then the reigning American champion over the mile—ran six laps around the audience, beating some other runners in the process. After winning the race, Dodds challenged his listeners: "I wonder how many of you here tonight are doing your best in the race for Jesus Christ". The sportsman's appearance apparently made a marked impact on the young people attending that night.[40]

Another major development in the 20th century was the establishment and growth of Christian sports organizations that aim to help Christian athletes to stand firm *in* their faith

---

40 Hoffman, 'Harvesting', p. 139; Ladd and Mathisen, pp. 96.

and to reach out *with* their faith. This has been particularly prominent in the Unites States. Sports Ambassadors (SA) was the first of these. In 1952 they employed the idea of top-quality Christian basketballers putting on an exhibition game in combination with personal testimonials and evangelistic talks by team members.[41] The idea proved a success. Soon afterwards, in 1954, the Fellowship of Christian Athletes (FCA) was founded, followed in 1966 by Athletes in Action (AIA).[42] While each of these organizations has a slightly different emphasis, the overall aim is to help believers to grow spiritually and to evangelize in both national and international contexts.

Christians in Sport commenced in the United Kingdom in the 1970s. Although not on as large a scale as their American counterparts, it has grown such that today it has thousands of supporters and works with churches and other partners in the UK and across the globe.[43] In Australia, 1984 saw the launch and development of Sports and Leisure Ministries (SLM). This organization had a particular focus on chaplaincy to sportsmen and women. And Australia, like other countries, developed more localized and sports-specific associations. For example, there are well-established ministries such as Christian Surfers Australia, along with more ad hoc groups such as a Sydney-based one called Christians in Cricket, with which I was involved in the 1990s.

---

41 Ladd and Mathisen, p. 127.
42 Hoffman, 'Harvesting Souls in the Stadium', p. 139; Ladd and Mathisen, pp. 127-35.
43 'History', *Christians in Sport UK:* christiansinsport.org.uk/about/history/.

The 1970s also saw the development of sports chaplaincies.[44] At the most general level, such chaplains seek to provide pastoral care to sportspeople—being concerned for their emotional, physical and spiritual needs. Chaplaincy has become increasingly organized with the formation of bodies such as Sports Chaplaincy Australia (formerly SLM).[45] Today, Christians serving in sports chaplaincy ministries can be found around the globe.

Sport on Sunday

While the question of whether sport should be played on Sundays has been an issue for many centuries, it has particularly come to the fore in the past hundred years with the rise of organized Sunday sport—both social and professional. As the 20th century progressed, Olympic events, baseball, football and cricket, for example, were increasingly played on this day of the week. These days it is almost impossible to avoid Sunday play at the top levels, as well as at many social levels.[46]

Many Christians have resisted this move. Early in the century, American baseball players such as Frank 'Home Run' Baker and Branch Rickey refused to play on Sunday.[47] Sprinter Eric Liddell famously refused to do the same in the 1924 Olympics. As the century progressed, however, there was

---

44 Ladd and Mathisen, p. 141.
45 'Services', *Sports Chaplaincy Australia*: sportschaplaincy.com.au/services.
46 Stuart Weir, *What the Book says about Sport*, The Bible Reading Fellowship, Oxford, 2000, p. 84.
47 Baker, pp. 158-9.

something of a shift, with evangelical Christians increasingly prepared to take part in Sunday play. Footballer Alan West captained Luton Town in the late 1970s and decided to play on the occasional Sunday. "I decided to play after giving it a lot of thought and prayer, realizing that it was my job, not just something I was doing for fun, and that I was under contract", he said. "I felt that if doctors and nurses, the police or bus drivers could do their jobs on a Sunday, what was the difference between them and me."[48]

Going against the modern trend, the great All Black rugby union flanker Michael Jones refused to play on Sundays.[49] But these days most evangelicals of almost all denominations would be open to Sunday sport so long as it doesn't conflict with church or at least regular Christian fellowship of some other sort. We will address what the Bible has to say on matters relevant to Sunday sport in chapter 11. The purpose here is simply to set out the historical trend.

Some negatives

While there have been many positives in the development of the Christianity-sport relationship, there have also been voices of concern. American historian William J Baker notes that two of the earliest beliefs of 'muscular Christians' were that sport was good for people both physically and morally. He suggests that, in modern sport, these two values "have become

---

48 Weir, pp. 87-8.
49 'Michael Jones (rugby union)', *Wikipedia*: en.wikipedia.org/wiki/Michael_Jones_(rugby_union).

muted, if not mangled beyond recognition".[50] Another to express his reservations is Shirl Hoffman, an American professor of exercise and sports science. Hoffman argues that the intellectual neglect of serious thinking about sport from a Christian perspective has led to the development of "an improbable sports theology"—*sportianity*—where the Bible is misused to support secular attitudes to sport.[51]

Another consequence of the purported lack of reflection on Christianity and sport is that many Christian sportspeople feel they are not sufficiently assisted in how to think about participating in sport as believers. A survey of students at a Christian college in the United States revealed that 86 percent who played in church league sports said they had received no instruction from their churches regarding how Christians should play sports.[52]

One of the goals of this book is to provide such instruction! It seeks to help Christian sportspeople (of any level), along with those Christians with an interest in sport, to think and reflect wisely on sport from a biblical perspective, and to be alert to the very real opportunities and dangers that sport brings.

It is very helpful to learn lessons from history. But, to be best equipped to take advantage of the opportunities and avoid the dangers, it is our relationship with God that is crucial. This is the topic of our next chapter.

---

50 Baker, p. 253.
51 Hoffman, *Good Game*, pp. 13-14 (quote from p. 14).
52 Hoffman, *Good Game*, p. 19.

THE CHRISTIAN SPORTSPERSON
Living with and for God on and off the field

> "But seek first his kingdom and his righteousness, and all these things will be given to you as well." (Matthew 6:33)

He was known as the 'Flying Scotsman'. In the early 1920s, Eric Liddell absolutely dominated the Scottish athletics scene. His preferred distances were the shorter sprints, which he ran full throttle, arms and legs pumping, his head thrown back in an unorthodox manner. He won the 100 yards and 220 yards at the 1923 AAA Championships in London, marking him out as the best sprinter in the UK.

But Eric did not just compete in athletics; he also featured in the backline of Scotland's rugby union side, studied Pure Science at the University of Edinburgh, and was heavily involved with Christian ministry—attending Morningside Congregational Church and speaking regularly for the Glasgow Students' Evangelistic Union at venues around the country.

Athletics was important to Eric—he trained hard under the guidance of Tom McKerchar, one of the leading coaches of the day. And when he competed, he did his best, once admitting "I don't like to be beaten".[1] But as much as he loved it, running was not the most important thing in Eric's life. He was first and foremost committed to following Christ.

His faith influenced everything, including his priorities, his character and his sport. He possessed a winsome personality and competed in a sportsmanlike matter. He shook hands with competitors before a race, ran hard (usually winning), and displayed humility afterwards. And, born to Scottish missionaries in China, his long-term goal in life was to return to that country and engage in missionary service.

As the 1924 Olympic Games in Paris drew closer, Eric, on form, would clearly have been one of the favourites for the 100 metres and 200 metres sprints. However, about half a year out from the games, he learned that the heats for the 100 metres were to be held on a Sunday. Eric's understanding of the Bible was that Sunday was the Lord's Day and was not a day for competing in sports.[2] As a result, he decided to withdraw from the 100 metres.

This shocked many members of the public and many in the press, not to mention the British Olympic Association. Significant pressure was put on him to change his mind, but Eric stood firm in his convictions. Eric and his coach decided

---

1   Hamilton, p. 85.
2   The historical issue of whether to play sport on Sunday was discussed briefly in chapter 2. We will consider this issue in more detail in chapter 11.

to redirect his training and focus on the 400 metres. This longer race requires a very different sort of preparation to that for the shorter sprints, with stamina as well as speed being needed.

Eventually the Paris Olympics came and, to the surprise of some, Eric performed well in the preliminary races, reaching the final but being placed in the outside lane. This is a difficult lane in which to run. With the staggered start, you run most of the race in front of your other competitors, with little idea of how you are going until you hit the final straight. Not many people considered him to have much of a chance.

Before the race, as was his practice, he shook the hands of all the other competitors. The gun went off. Eric started quickly and, against conventional wisdom, set a blistering pace in the first 200 metres. He maintained his speed longer than expected and was still in front when the runners reached the final straight. Most assumed he would fade and be overtaken by the more experienced 400-metre runners, but he just kept going—head back, arms and legs pumping like pistons. He was first to the tape in a world record time of 47.6 seconds. Interviewed after the race, Eric said, "The secret of my success over the 400 metres is that I run the first 200 metres as hard as I can. Then, for the second 200 metres, with God's help, I run harder."[3] Eric returned to British shores a national hero.

A bright future of athletic success and further Olympic glory beckoned, but Eric stuck to his priorities and plan. "I

---

[3] Russell W Ramsay, *God's Joyful Runner: The Family-authorised Biography of Eric Liddell: Hero of the Movie Chariots of Fire*, Bridge, South Plainfield, 1987, p. 68.

believe God made me for China", he often repeated.⁴ In accordance with his great desire, he returned to that country to join his family in missionary service in 1925. There he served in various capacities—as a teacher, preacher, pastor, and in other practical ways. Sport was not absent from his life, though. He taught it at school, and sometimes engaged in local athletic competitions.

China was not a safe place at this time, with warring Chinese factions, a strong anti-British sentiment, and eventually a Japanese invasion. Life could be cheap, and Eric's was often in great danger. In 1943, he was placed in a Japanese civilian internment camp. Here, in filthy, confined and deprived conditions, the health and morale of internees was placed under great strain. Factions and fights were common. Amidst all this, however, Eric set about teaching, preaching, pastoring, and organizing athletic events for the many children in the camp. He was greatly loved, his Christian character standing up to the rigors of this Spartan existence. One fellow internee later wrote that he was "overflowing with good humour and love of life", and possessed "enthusiasm and charm". As he recalled, "It is rare indeed when a person has the good fortune to meet a saint, but he came as close to it as anyone I have ever known".⁵

In 1945, Eric's health declined, and on 21 February he died from a brain tumour, bringing grief to his family and fellow internees. As the caption at the end of the movie *Chariots of*

---

4   Hamilton, p. 125.
5   Langdon Gilkey, *Shantung Compound: The story of men and women under pressure*, Harper & Row, New York, 1975, p. 192.

Fire announces, "All of Scotland mourned."⁶ To this day he is still one of that country's most popular sportsmen.

A Christian... who plays sport

As Christians, like Liddell, we are Christians who play sport, not sportspeople who happen to be Christians. With God's help, we seek to put Christ first in our lives. Following Jesus is our priority, and it should be a wholehearted commitment. In light of the gospel outlined in the early chapters of his letter to the Romans, Paul writes:

> **Therefore, I urge you, brothers and sisters, in view of God's mercy, to offer your bodies as a living sacrifice, holy and pleasing to God—this is your true and proper worship. (Rom 12:1)**

Thankfully, we are not in this alone. In all areas of Christian living—including in all those things the Scriptures would urge us to do as set out in this book—we labour with the strength that God provides (e.g. Phil 2:12-13; Col 1:29).

This idea of wholehearted devotion may be unnerving for some. It means our lives as Christians are no longer our own—they belong to the Lord. He, not the sporting calendar, sets our agenda. But as we noted in chapter 1, we have nothing to fear from someone who loves us so much that "he gave his one and only Son" for us (John 3:16). In addition, God also has

---

6 Much of the information about Liddell in this section came from Hamilton's *For the Glory,* Ramsay's *God's Joyful Runner,* and from Wikipedia's page on Eric Liddell: wikipedia.org/wiki/Eric_Liddell.

great plans for us: "For we are God's handiwork, created in Christ Jesus to do good works, which God prepared in advance for us to do" (Eph 2:10). These plans might mean that we end up playing more sport, or they might mean that we end up playing less sport. In either case, his plans for us and what he might do through us are always good.

This means that to whatever extent we are involved with sport, our Christian faith impacts all aspects of it. Our faith impacts not just what we do on Sundays, but also what we do from Monday to Saturday. It impacts not just our church involvement, but also our family, work, rest, study—and our sport.

Andrew Wingfield Digby was the sports-mad son of an English vicar. Converted in his late teens, he went on to represent Oxford and Combined Universities in the 1970s in cricket, become a vicar, and help launch Christians in Sport in the UK. Over the years, he has learned to integrate sport into his Christian life. But this was not always the case. "As a new Christian I saw no real connection between sport and my Christian faith", he recalls. "It was like something I did when I was 'off duty'. I thought how nice it was that God let me play it. I had no real understanding of how sport was a gift from God, or of how it could actually be part of my Christian ministry."

Our relationship with God will affect how we think about sport, how we play sport, and how we treat and behave with the people with whom we come into contact through sport. Everything—sport included—is done for God. As Paul writes: "Whatever you do, work at it with all your heart, as working for the Lord, not for human masters" (Col 3:23). Living this way will bring glory to God, is best for others, and is best for ourselves.

Connecting with the Coach

Clearly, a healthy relationship with God is absolutely crucial to living life in a Christian way on and off the field. Accordingly, we need to work at maintaining it.

Jesus speaks of the importance of this relationship in his teaching about the vine and branches in John 15:

> "I am the vine; you are the branches. If you remain in me and I in you, you will bear much fruit; apart from me you can do nothing. If you do not remain in me, you are like a branch that is thrown away and withers; such branches are picked up, thrown into the fire and burned. If you remain in me and my words remain in you, ask whatever you wish, and it will be done for you. This is to my Father's glory, that you bear much fruit, showing yourselves to be my disciples.
>
> "As the Father has loved me, so have I loved you. Now remain in my love. If you keep my commands, you will remain in my love, just as I have kept my Father's commands and remain in his love. I have told you this so that my joy may be in you and that your joy may be complete." (John 15:5-11)

We need to remain in Jesus like a branch remains in a vine. This metaphor highlights the closeness of the relationship, which is also a loving and joyful one (vv. 9, 11), and which allows us to "bear much fruit" (v. 8). *Fruit* might be understood as actions and attributes that bring glory to God. In the realm of sport, this might include doing one's best, displaying good sportsmanship, finding opportunities to encourage other believers we play with and against, and taking opportunities to bear witness to our faith when with non-believers.

Maintaining a strong relationship with God will help us to survive and thrive in the faith as we face the many challenges and temptations that can arise both on and off the field. British Olympic rower Debbie Flood reflects on how helpful her faith was in navigating her sporting career:

> It was such a blessing to become a Christian before I really became immersed in the world of sport. My faith was such a massive anchor in a world that could sometimes be so selfish, in which there was the constant danger of having my identity caught up in sport, and in which it was so easy to go from hero to zero overnight.

Bible reading and prayer

To stand firm as a Christian, to grow as a Christian, to play sport in a godly way, to enjoy sport in the way God intended, and to have a positive impact on those around us (in the sporting context and otherwise), we must constantly listen to God's word and pray to him. In the same way that an athlete-coach relationship thrives when there is good communication, so too our relationship with the ultimate Super-coach thrives on good communication.

This communication flows both ways—a point we've already seen Jesus make in John 15. Remaining in him involves his words remaining in us (v. 7a). This means not simply reading the Bible, but meditating deeply on it and putting it into practice, allowing God's word to shape the way that we live. And as we do this, we should speak to the Lord in prayer, asking him about "whatever [we] wish" (v. 7b).

Life is a spiritual battle, and to fight it we need spiritual weapons such as these (Eph 6:10-20). Look at how the psalmist writes about God's word:

> Blessed is the one
> who does not walk in step with the wicked
> or stand in the way that sinners take
> or sit in the company of mockers,
> but whose delight is in the law of the LORD,
> and who meditates on his law day and night. (Ps 1:1-2)[7]

As for prayer, Paul urges the people of God to "devote yourselves to prayer" and "pray continually" (Col 4:2; 1 Thess 5:17). The Lord Jesus himself taught his disciples "that they should always pray and not give up" (Luke 18:1).

The Bible teaches of the need to meditate on Scripture and to pray on a daily basis. One very helpful practice is to set aside time each day to read and reflect on the Bible and to pray to God. This is something I have always sought to do, and it has helped me greatly.

Susie Harris would agree. Susie was something of a hockey prodigy. As a 12-year-old, she was playing regional under-18s hockey. By age 17, she had made the Australian team for the 2002 World Cup in Perth, and went on to represent her country on over 50 occasions. Her success in sport meant she was often away from home and mixing with women who were much older than she. Significantly, Susie was a Christian, and God, through Susie's parents, had prepared her well for life in this sort of environment. "We were a Christian and church-

---

[7] For more on the nature of God's word, see Romans 10:17, Colossians 3:16, 2 Timothy 3:16-17, and Hebrews 2:1.

going family", she says. "As I was growing up, my parents talked to me about the Christian faith. They said that Christian living was counter-cultural living. They also explained to me the importance of walking daily with Jesus through Bible reading and prayer. Communicating with God in this way became a day-to-day habit for me. I'd do this when I was at home; I'd do it when I was away. In fact, being away from home—a Christian in a non-Christian context—helped me to grow in my faith. Having no-one else, I fell back on the Lord as my best friend. As I read the Bible and talked to the Lord each day, my faith and trust in him grew."

If you are not in the habit of having a daily time of Bible reading and prayer, why not resolve to begin now?

Church and Christian fellowship

Meeting regularly with other Christians is the other chief way we grow in our faith. The writer of Hebrews urges:

> **And let us consider how we may spur one another on toward love and good deeds, not giving up meeting together, as some are in the habit of doing, but encouraging one another—and all the more as you see the Day approaching. (Heb 10:24-25)**

When we meet together in church, we hear God's word read and taught, we pray to our Heavenly Father, we praise God in song, and we have the opportunity to encourage and spur one another on in our Christian lives. Meeting regularly with other Christians in church, in fellowship groups, in Bible study groups, at training courses, at Christian conventions and in other social contexts can also be very refreshing. I have always loved meeting with keen believers, and the apostle Paul must have felt similarly—he writes of hoping to visit the Christians in Rome so that he might "be refreshed" in their company (Rom 15:32).

The Christian relationships that I witnessed and was part of at church and youth group when I was growing up were such that I *wanted* to live as a Christian. I did not want to behave in the way that my non-Christian sporting friends sometimes did. I did not want to get drunk, have sex before marriage, or look at pornography. I was convinced that living the Christian way did not just bring glory to God and was better for others—it was also better for me.

Do you attend church each week? Are you involved in regular fellowship? This is particularly important given the potentially consuming nature of sport. I once asked the former Australian volleyball captain Priscilla Ruddle how she sought to stand firm and grow as a Christian when she was playing competitive sport. Her response: "By having a good church base, including involvement in weekly Bible study, attending a prayer meeting at the Australian Institute of Sport, having close Christian friends who were willing to keep me accountable, and access to chaplains."

But what if sport clashes with church? Or what if it regularly takes you away from home on tours, thus making weekly church attendance or regular fellowship difficult? This is a topic we will address further in chapter 11. Whatever your view, it is essential to have access to regular Bible teaching and fellowship.

If sport is played on a Sunday morning, and you think there are good Christian reasons for your playing that sport, then go to church on a Sunday afternoon or evening. If sport takes you interstate or overseas for a period of time, arrange to be involved with a church in that location. When Susie Harris moved from Sydney to Perth to attend the Australian Institute of Sport, her parents organized for her to live with a Christian family, and Susie started attending a local church. I know of other parents who organized a midweek Christian youth group so that their hockey-playing daughter could have regular fellowship with people her age.

For some who play sport at a higher level, schedules can be a little more erratic. With games or competitions sometimes taking place on Sundays, their church lifestyle is a little like that experienced by Christians who are employed as shiftworkers. Linvoy Primus became a Christian while playing English Premier League football for Portsmouth at the start of this century. He began attending a local church but found he could not get there every week. However, his club—as do many major sporting clubs—had a chaplain, and he made a point of meeting with him each week for Bible study and prayer. Now retired from the game, Linvoy notes that those footballers who get involved with local churches—even if they are not able to get there on a weekly basis—are less likely to drift in their faith.

While our personal circumstances will all be different, the key principle is to put Christ first in our lives. This will involve prioritizing personal Bible reading and prayer, and maintaining regular Christian teaching and fellowship. In addition, there are many other things we can do to help us stand firm and grow in our relationship with God—for example, we can read Christian books, download Christian talks, listen to Christian music, and watch Christian videos.

Relational breakdown

Relational strain and breakdown is always sad and often devastating for people. Rifts between players and coaches, or between players and other players, are numerous and have been well documented. Worse still are relational strains and breakdowns within the family. And while it often may not feel like it, the worst form of relational strain and disengagement that can occur is in our relationship with God. It is so serious because it involves God himself, and because it detrimentally affects all our other relationships, as well as our own personal wellbeing. Though sport is a good thing, there is always the danger that it can be misused so that it damages our relationship with God. Our commitment to it in terms of time, relationships and emotional focus can be such that our relationship with God is squeezed out.

When our relationship with God grows distant, damage results—God is not glorified, it is bad for others, and it is bad for us. If we realize that we are falling into this trap, now is a good time to turn back to God—to re-engage. The apostle Peter grew distant from Jesus—but then came back, and God used him to achieve great things. This has happened with millions of Christians since then. And it can be true for you!

Two key battlegrounds

If our relationship with God remains strongly intact, we can stand firm in the faith, and God can use us to advance his kingdom. Before looking into this more in coming chapters, we will briefly consider two key battlegrounds often found in off-the-field sporting culture—alcohol and sexual morality. In both these areas, Christians can either set a wonderful example or display tragic compromise, making it vital that we sustain a close relationship with our 'Super-coach'.

Alcohol

This is a big one. The consumption of alcohol is a significant part of many sporting cultures. The victories of elite sporting teams are often associated with media images of champagne bottles shaken and sprayed, beers downed in sweaty change rooms, and worse-for-wear players after post-win 'big nights out'. The same can often be said of sporting teams much further down the spectrum, although in their case images are unlikely to appear on anything other than social media. I recall hearing a victory speech from a player in a suburban football team in which he referred to the training his team did on Thursday nights down at the pub (or something like that). I have played cricket in both Australia and England and can testify that, in both contexts, the consumption of beer was a significant part of time spent together after the game and on nights out. My teammates varied from those who drank very little to those who drank an awful lot.

The Bible clearly teaches that we should avoid getting drunk. Ephesians 5:18 instructs: "Do not get drunk on wine, which leads to debauchery. Instead, be filled with the Spirit…" Being drunk is disobedient to God, does not bring glory to God, can cause great damage to other people, and can harm the drinker. For regular drinkers, there is the threat of becoming addicted and all the personal tragedy associated with that.

How many sportspeople can we think of who have struggled here?

When I was about 18, I decided that I would never have more than two alcoholic drinks on any one occasion. Over the years, this has meant that I can be social in this way if I wish, but with clear limits set for myself I have managed to retain self-control. My perception, both in Australian and England sporting contexts, has been that people have appreciated that I wanted to spend time with them, but understood that because I was a Christian I was not prepared to get drunk.

You may like to adopt a similar practice yourself. However, it should be noted that I am 194 centimetres tall (6'4"). If you are of a different size, you might decide to set a different limit. Furthermore, I am very self-disciplined by nature. If that is not you, and you are someone who is unable to stick to your limits, it would probably be best for you to avoid drinking altogether. Another thing to consider is whether our drinking is likely to tempt another person to drink too much—in which case it would be best to abstain on such occasions. We need to think about not just our own limits but also the temptations that others face. This is particularly the case when we are with other Christians. As Paul writes, "It is better not to eat meat or drink wine or to do anything else that will cause your brother or sister to fall" (Rom 14:21).

Sexual morality

In the Sermon on the Mount, Jesus teaches:

> "You have heard that it was said, 'You shall not commit adultery.' But I tell you that anyone who looks at a woman lustfully has already committed adultery with her in his heart." (Matt 5:27-28)

Given that we can commit sexual immorality with our thoughts as well as our actions, the temptation is widespread and very real, and can arise in many forms. It might be looking at the athletic figure of another sportsperson and allowing our mind to travel in unhelpful directions. It might be access to pornography—for example, the passing around of pornographic magazines, or an invitation to a 'prawn and porn' night. It might be access to willing sexual partners other than our spouse—whether they be other sportspeople, or people met at parties or during nights out on the town. For the famous, there is the additional challenge that there are often people who specifically seek out sexual encounters with celebrities.

Again, we need to realize and be convinced that engaging in sexual immorality is disobedient to God, does not bring glory to God, and can cause great damage to other people, as well as harming ourselves. It is best to avoid situations where we know that we might be genuinely tempted, and if we find ourselves in a situation where our desires are getting the better of us we need to get out of there as quickly as we can. As Paul writes: "Flee from sexual immorality" (1 Cor 6:18).

But this area it not just one where there are dangers to avoid. It is one where we can present a positive alternative.

We can show genuine friendship to other sportspeople who may happen to have attractive figures or personalities. We can treat them with love, respect, and "absolute purity" (1 Tim 5:2). We can avoid all contact with pornography. In this way, our interactions and relationships can be positive and God-honouring. It might also make our friends stop and think.

I enjoyed playing a season of cricket in England as a young man in my early 20s, and made many good friends at the club for which I played. This, of course, meant that there was a lot of good-natured banter in the dressing room, with people trying to wind me up. One teammate liked asking me on a regular basis: "Liggo, did you get a bit of crumpet last night?" (He was not referring to that item usually cooked by bakers.) I would usually respond with something along the lines of: "Well, I went out with some friends from church to a movie, and then we ended up singing songs, praying and chatting on someone's living room floor until about midnight." I remember someone—I think it was the same guy—quizzing me about sex. "So, Liggo, you say you're not going to have sex until you're married." I agreed that that was my intention. To my surprise, he did not ridicule me. In fact, he looked somewhat wistful.

The areas of alcohol and sexual morality can bring significant temptation. However, like all areas of our sporting lives, they are also ones which provide us with a great opportunity for honouring God and for personal witness—*if* our relationship with God is strong.

Stay connected

David Simmons scored over 100 first grade tries in the Australian National Rugby League. Throughout this time, he was a follower of Jesus. "I became a Christian a couple of years before I started rising through the ranks," he says, "so I was growing a lot as a Christian and progressing as a footballer at the same time". This helped him to negotiate the highs and lows of football, to grasp the opportunities, and to avoid the dangers associated with the game.

A particularly difficult period, when his team was struggling and he was dropped from first grade, drove David deeper into the Scriptures. He came to a greater appreciation of God's sovereignty and the fact that God could work through suffering with a view to making him more like Christ and preparing him for eternal life. "There is a real peace and joy in knowing that God is there in all circumstances of life, that every moment is under his sovereign care and control, and that our eternal future is guaranteed by God's grace."

And what helped him in his relationship with God throughout his career? "Really, the same things that have helped God's people for centuries—I read my Bible regularly, prayed, went to church, and tried to live a life following Jesus."

If we are Christians, we are Christians who, amongst other things, may play sport. Loving God with all our heart, soul, mind and strength, and loving our neighbours as ourselves will (and must) be our priority (Mark 12:30-31). Sport can be a real plus as we seek to do this—or it can be a real minus. The key thing is to stay connected with the Coach.

THE JOY OF SPORT

Sport's intrinsic value

**In the heavens God has pitched a tent for the sun.
It is like a bridegroom coming out of his chamber,
like a champion rejoicing to run his course.
(Psalm 19:4b-5)**

///

It was a cold night in Melbourne when the Australian women's hockey team (the reigning Olympic champions) took on the might of China (the holders of the Champion's Trophy) in the Oceania Cup. Susie Harris was 18, had only been part of the national squad for a year, and was still getting used to playing at this level. Partway through the second half, Australia moved the play quickly down the right-hand side of the field. Susie, one of the strikers, started to run into position near the edge of the circle. When one of her teammates put in the cross, Susie was ready and slammed it first time into the bottom left-hand corner of the goal. "It was one of those perfect moments," Susie says, "a moment of pure joy—the culmination of years of training, when everything goes right in an almost perfect way". Within seconds, she was swamped by teammates offering their congratulations.

A few years later on the far side of the globe, Linvoy Primus was playing in the defence for Portsmouth FC in the English Premier League against footballing powerhouse Manchester United. United's embarrassment of superstars included England's goal-scoring machine Wayne Rooney. During a crucial stage of the game, Rooney had the ball and was heading for goal. Linvoy found himself in a position where he may have been able to reach his opponent in the penalty area and prevent his run and possible shot on goal. But if he mistimed the tackle, he risked giving away a penalty and perhaps being sent off. He had only a few seconds to decide what to do. "I made the decision [to attempt the tackle], got to Rooney in the box, and with a perfectly timed slide took ball and man at exactly the same time. It was a legal tackle. A goal was saved." Another moment of sporting joy.

But the joys of sport are not limited to top-flight sportspeople. Far from it. The majority of sporting enjoyment takes place at the more everyday level with people who are not famous, taking part in local competitions such as the weeknight netball competition or the Saturday morning park run.

Nor are the thrills of sport limited to successful results. There is also the sheer joy of taking part. Former England under-21 hockey player Elizabeth Chambers describes the satisfaction she gained from playing her favourite game. "It was such a buzz to be around the other players and to be part of the team", she says. "Playing hockey made me feel really alive—and playing well was such a thrill. I loved pushing myself to the limit in games, and waking up the next day feeling totally ruined." Australian long-distance runner Eloise Wellings describes the joy of running: "I feel free when I run. It's liberating. It clears the head and gives me the opportunity to think and dream."

We can experience the joy of sport in many ways. There is the sudden thrill of scoring a goal, the immersive experience of a keenly fought contest, and the more prolonged satisfaction of looking back on a season well played or a career now concluded. There are the hours spent training for a sporting encounter, the anticipation of its commencement, the excitement of being out there, and the pleasure of reflecting back on it afterwards. There is the physical, mental and technical challenge, the thrill of competition, the enjoyment of relationships, the release from the everyday, and the feeling of physical wellbeing. And, aside from first-hand involvement, there is the pleasure of watching sport, reading about sport, and following your favourite player or team. In so many ways, sport engages the mind, body and emotions.

The joy of participation

As the examples just mentioned illustrate, sport can be the source of great joy. This truth is something that millions upon millions have taken to heart. The Bible itself recognizes this possibility. King David writes in Psalm 19:

> In the heavens God has pitched a tent for the sun.
> > It is like a bridegroom coming out of his chamber,
> > like a champion rejoicing to run his course. (Ps 19:4b-5)

In speaking of how the wonders of creation point to God, David compares the rising of the sun to a man who has just been married, and the path of the sun across the sky to a champion running a course. The runner rejoices in his athletic expression.

Ashley Null is a world-renowned scholar on the theology of the English Reformation. More significantly for our purposes, he also serves as a chaplain to elite athletes, including serving at three separate Olympic Games. This has given him numerous opportunities to observe sport and sportspeople. "Yes, sport is special", he says. "It makes your body feel good. It makes you feel good about yourself. It makes you feel good about your life. It even gives you friends it feels good to be with. Very few things in life can claim to offer as much joy as sport does."[1]

The joy of observation

The joys of sport are not limited to participation—there is also the joy of observation. Ian Wooldridge of London's *Daily Mail* was one of the most celebrated sports journalists of the 20th century. He loved the fact that his job allowed him to watch sport for free. He once described his profession as "an equable arrangement under which a newspaper pays you for doing what you would have done anyway, had you been born rich. I cannot imagine a more pleasant way of passing one's time on

---

1 John Ashley Null, *Real Joy: Freedom to be your Best*, Hänssler Verlag & SRS Pro Sportler, Holzgerlingen & Altenkirchen, 2005, p. 4.

this planet."[2]

It's not just watching world-class sport that can focus our attention. Most parents get great joy out of watching their children play sport—mastering a skill, working with a team, displaying good sportsmanship, achieving a level of success. I remember a friend of mine describing how his heart "swelled with pride" as he watched one of his sons perform well on the sporting field. And for the true sports-lover, joy can be obtained by stopping and watching almost anyone playing on a local field or court given half an excuse and opportunity.

...and the frustration and disappointment

Of course, lest we paint an unrealistically rosy picture, the world of sport is *not* one of unceasing and ever-increasing joy. We live in a fallen world where bad things happen, where bad character is displayed (by us and others), and where our bodies sometimes simply refuse to do the things we ask of them. There are the perversions of sport that we will talk about throughout this book, but there are also the day-to-day disappointments and frustrations of simply having a bad day on the court, losing, or being unable to successfully refine some technical aspect of our game. This may often be followed by returning to form, a victory, or *eventually* mastering that skill—but not always! We may never emerge from the slump,

---

[2] Ian Wooldridge, 'Hunt, Klammer, Idi Amin, Mary Peters, Dexter, Barrington', in David Lord (ed.), *The Glory of Sport: Indelible Stories from Ten of the World's Best Sportswriters*, Frost, Kurralta Park, 1979, p. 11.

never beat that team, or never get that movement right; we may simply have reached our limits. Sport will not always *feel* joyful. It is a mixture.

Thinking about, thanking, and glorifying God

As we said in the previous chapter, our sporting and spiritual lives are not mutually exclusive spheres. Everything with which we are involved—church, family, work, study and sport—is part of our spiritual life. The all-inclusive nature of following Jesus is seen in Colossians 3:23: "*Whatever you do*, work at it with all your heart, as working for the Lord, not for human masters". Note this: "*whatever* you do", God is relevant to it.

Thinking about God

Thinking about God when we are involved with sport can be easier said than done. It is sadly possible for us to go for extended periods of time without ever once thinking of our Lord and Saviour, let alone communicating with him, or considering how our being children of God impacts what we are doing. This can certainly be true with sport. But there are some habits that can help.

I have played a few seasons of football in a local church league. A regular practice in these games was for both teams to meet in the middle of the field to pray before the start of the game. The degree to which different players engaged with the prayers varied, but it did remind us all that God was part of what we were about to do for the next 90 minutes.

Most sporting contests, however, do not provide these sorts

of opportunities, so we have to remind ourselves of God's presence. Stuart Weir, Executive Director of Verité Sport in the UK (an organization that seeks to promote the integration of Christianity and sport), recounts the practice of Jamaican dual Olympic gold medal winning sprinter Shelly-Ann Fraser-Pryce. "When she was on the blocks," he says, "she'd often recite a Bible verse. And after she finished a race she made a point of smiling to express gratitude to God for the opportunity to run."

One of the things I did for many years was to pray throughout the day when I played cricket. I would offer a short prayer before running in to bowl and before facing a delivery when batting. Another of my practices for a while was to carry a Bible around in my cricket bag. I did not usually read my Bible *at* the cricket game, but its presence there reminded me—and potentially others—of God and of my Christian faith.

Thanking God

So we should think about God when we compete, but what exactly should we be thinking of? There are many possibilities, but an important starting point would be to *thank God* for our sport. Paul writes to Timothy: "For everything God created is good, and nothing is to be rejected if it is received with thanksgiving" (1 Tim 4:4). As we've already seen, sport is a good gift from God and, accordingly, should be received with thanksgiving.

We can thank God that the sport we are playing was invented, and that we have the body, ability, time, money and fellow competitors that allow us to play the sport. There was a period in human history when our favourite sport did not exist. And there are many people who, for all kinds of reasons, are unable to play that sport. We are fortunate to live at a time and place in human history when participation is even possible. Not to thank God for the opportunity to participate would make us like the spoilt child who does not appreciate how much his parents have given him.

Some people are also especially gifted in a particular sport. Many top-class sportspeople recognize that this gifting comes from God and that he needs to be thanked for it. Former South African cricket captain and all-rounder Shaun Pollock once told me: "I know that I've been given talent by God and I've got to use it to his glory". Many other Christian sportspeople have drawn similar conclusions.

Glorifying God

As well as thinking of God and thanking God, we can also—as Shaun Pollock has noted—use sport to *glorify God*. We often hear sportspeople say after a sporting performance in which they do well that they "give all the glory to God". (Some may cynically wonder if the person would give glory to God if they had not done so well. But, to be fair, the media do not usually interview those who are less successful.) But what does it mean to glorify God? And can we glorify God in ways other than actually saying "we glorify God"?

To give glory to God means to speak and act in a way that gives honour to God, and which reflects his greatness. It involves words:

> Ascribe to the LORD, all you families of nations,
>   ascribe to the LORD glory and strength.
> Ascribe to the LORD the glory due his name...
>   (1 Chr 16:28-29a)

It also involves actions:

> So whether you eat or drink or whatever you do, do it all for the glory of God. (1 Cor 10:31)

A sportsperson can glorify God with their words by acknowledging that the ability and opportunity to play their sport, regardless of how they perform, comes ultimately from God. Thus, athletes might thank God or give glory to God when they perform well or when they simply participate.

We can also glorify God in our actions. Australian brother and sister pairs figure skaters Stephen and Danielle Carr competed at three Winter Olympics in the 1990s. Stephen once commented that he and Danielle would often pray with each other, especially as they grew older. Their prayers about their skating also changed as they matured in their Christian faith. When they were younger believers, Stephen prayed that God would help them to win the competitions in which they were competing. As his faith developed, they prayed that God would strengthen them and that they would "skate for the glory of God".

How can a performance bring honour to God? First, a sportsperson can bring glory to God simply by using their God-given gift. Former Chelsea and Newcastle Premier League footballer Gavin Peacock has said, "I regard my ability to play football as a gift from God. He has given me the talent.

I believe he wants me to work hard and make the best of what he has given me and use it for his glory."[3]

Sometimes the quality of a sporting performance is such that it takes the breath away and points to the power, creativity and beauty of God. Of course, God's power, creativity and beauty are far beyond anything that a mere sporting performance can achieve, but it can give us a glimpse. A Christian sportsperson performing the athletic feat might be aware that this is what they are doing. A non-Christian performing the athletic feat would not be aware. But in either case, the Christian spectator can appreciate it. I sat near the final baton change for the 4 x 100 metres relay finals at the Sydney Olympics in 2000. The sight of the runners hurtling around the bend at incredible speed and then fluidly passing the baton to the next runners was awe-inspiring. The power, pace and precision of the process took my breath away, and certainly pointed to the qualities of the God who created all this.

Second, a sportsperson can bring glory to God by the way in which they participate—for example, by doing their best, and by displaying good sportsmanship. Colossians 3:23, cited earlier, says: "Whatever you do, *work at it with all your heart*, as working for the Lord, not for human masters". Dual Olympic gold medal winning South African breaststroker Penny Heyns has spoken of how she came to appreciate that swimming laps of the pool was an opportunity for her to worship God. "I committed to giving my whole being and heart to God in every moment of my swimming", she

---

3   Weir, p. 32.

says.[4] And while we will discuss sportsmanship more in the next chapter, it must be said here that competing in a sportsmanlike manner brings great glory to God and shows us something of his love.

It would be a tragedy for all concerned if a Christian participating in sport did not think of God when playing sport, thank God for that sport, and seek to bring glory to God in that sport by their words and actions.

When good becomes god—the danger of idolatry

It would be nice if we could finish the chapter here. Unfortunately, the problem is that sport, like all things, is damaged by sin. As we noted in chapter 1, one of the things sinful human nature can cause us to do is to turn a good thing like sport into a 'God thing'. This is idolatry—putting something else in the place of God. It is a very common sin, and one that has been around for a long time.

Back in the Old Testament, God spoke of idolatry in the Ten Commandments:

> "You shall not make for yourself an image in the form of anything in heaven above or on the earth beneath or in the waters below. You shall not bow down to them or worship them…" (Exod 20:4-5a)

We may think that this is hardly our problem today. Most of us

---

[4] Penny Heyns, 'Training Worship', in Josh Davis (ed.), *The Goal and the Glory: World-class Athletes Share their Inspiring Stories*, Regal, Ventura, 2008, p. 71.

in the West do not worship carved or moulded idols. However, the New Testament makes clear that we may worship—or put first—things other than God. Romans 1:25 describes how people have "exchanged the truth about God for a lie, and worshiped and served created things rather than the Creator". And Colossians 3:5 urges: "Put to death, therefore, whatever belongs to your earthly nature: sexual immorality, impurity, lust, evil desires and greed, which is idolatry".

Idolatry is extremely common today, and sport is very often the idol. In the 1960s, the American runner Jim Ryun set world records in the 800 metres, 1500 metres, and the mile, winning a silver medal in the 1968 Olympics. Looking back, Ryun admits: "For 10 years, running was my god. I gave my god the best of everything—my time, my energy, my love."[5] This level of dedication and devotion is not that unusual and can be found the world over in sportspeople of all levels.

The tragedy is that sport makes a lousy god. It promises a lot but fails to deliver. Ryun, now a Christian, certainly found this. "At the age of 25, however, I realized something was missing in my life", he says. "According to the world's standards, I was very successful. I was the world record holder in the mile, had been on the cover of *Sports Illustrated* and still had many years of running left in my legs. Success according to the world's barometer was nice, but there was a great emptiness within me. No matter how fast I ran, people were always expecting more. No matter how many awards I won, I always wanted

---

5   Jim Ryun, 'Forgiven to Forgive', in Davis, *The Goal and the Glory*, p. 106.

more. There was no peace inside, and at times living seemed more like a roller-coaster ride than a rewarding journey."[6]

The same sort of obsession can be true of supporters. American academic Shirl Hoffman recounts the story of a Mr and Mrs Reece—fans of the University of Alabama's American football team. The couple had purchased a $300,000 motorhome exclusively for the purpose of travelling to Alabama's games. So enthused were they about supporting their team that they missed their daughter's wedding because it clashed with a big game. When asked about this, they pointed out that they had asked their daughter not to schedule the wedding at a time which conflicted with the match, and that they *had* managed to make the reception. When further asked about why he did it, Mr Reece admitted, "I just love Alabama football" and said it's "all I can think of".[7]

Not only does idolizing sport insult the one true God who ultimately created sport; the faulty commitment is also damaging to others and to one's self. Ashley Null eloquently describes the "loss of joy" that is experienced by so many athletes who view sport in this way. According to Null, the three joys of sport for children growing up are *release, relationships* and a *reputation*. It can be a great way to relax, form friendships, and be known as being good at something. However, when a boy or girl realizes they are good at a sport, there is the danger that the drive to create a reputation through athletic success can destroy sport as a means of release and squeeze out

---

6   Ryun, p. 106.
7   Hoffman, *Good Game*, p. 1.

relationships. If you are not winning, there is disappointment and the drive to train harder. If you keep on winning, the joy associated with success eventually fades. Athletes taking this path are on the road to burn out, which in turn causes many athletes to turn to three easy crutches for release—drinking, dating and casual sex. But, in the long term, these don't provide satisfaction either. "The inner passion of these elite athletes will burn through their makeshift fireplaces, leaving them burned out and those around them burned up."[8]

Idolatrous attitudes

As we noted in chapter 1, Christians cannot be guilty of idolatry as, by definition, Christians cannot have something other than God taking God's place in their lives. However, all Christian sportspeople will feel the pull of idolatrous attitudes at various times. Three very common dangers are selfish ambitions, unhelpful obsession, and finding one's personal significance and sense of self-identity in sport.

Selfish ambition

Most Christians will participate in sport at a fairly low-key and social level. Some, however, will take is very seriously, and a few will even pursue it at a professional level. Wanting to do well, and perhaps aiming to get somewhere with our sport, is not a bad thing, but we will need to go about it in a godly way. We will want to train hard and do our best, then accept

---

8   Null, pp. 6-20 (quotes from pp. 12, 20).

the results that God sends us—displaying humility in victory and graciousness in defeat. We need to treat those with whom we play—both teammates and opposition—with respect. We respect our opponents by doing our best against them, playing by the rules, and displaying good sportsmanship (the topic of our next chapter).

Trying our best is not the problem; selfish ambition is the problem. Paul writes: "Do nothing out of selfish ambition or vain conceit. Rather, in humility value others above yourselves" (Phil 2:3). A danger for some sportspeople is that we can become so caught up in our own performance that we struggle to respect others or to show humility and graciousness. Living in a godly way in this area can be a challenge, but God can help us. The key thing is to work on our relationship with God—to "remain in the vine" (John 15:4).

Unhelpful obsession

It is good to enjoy thinking about sport, planning training programs, working on our technique, doing things that will enable us to improve. It is also good to enjoy reading about sport and following particular teams. But whether playing or supporting, we don't want this interest or focus to become unhelpfully obsessive. Some personalities are more prone to this than others, as perhaps were those University of Alabama supporters referred to earlier. At various points, I've worked hard at refining the subtleties of my bowling action or my shot put delivery. Occasionally, I've wondered whether my focus has bordered on the unhelpfully excessive. It can be a fine line. Again, the key here is to work on our relationship with God.

Personal significance and self-identity

As Christians, we find our identity and significance in the fact that we are created by God and loved by God, not in the fact that we play or may be good at sport. Genesis tells us:

> So God created mankind in his own image,
> in the image of God he created them;
> male and female he created them. (Gen 1:27)

Whoever we are and however good at sport we are, we are created in the image of God. John 3:16 tells us that God loves us so much "that he gave his one and only Son" for us. We are loved by God to an unimaginable degree. And, as believers, we are adopted into God's family (Rom 8:13-17; Gal 4:4-7)!

Our personal significance and identity are found in Christ. This is such an important truth for Christian sportspeople to grasp. But for many of us, a real temptation is to find our identity, to some extent, in our sport and our sporting successes. This tendency dishonours God and makes life unnecessarily hard for us. Sport is notorious for having its ups and downs—if our identity is not firmly rooted in Christ, we can take a real battering.

As I've said, I had hopes of becoming a professional cricketer when younger. But a combination of injury and technical flaws held me back, and by the age of 22 I realized that I was not going to make it. I was very disappointed—nothing wrong with that. But I started to realize that, even though I sought to put God first in my life, a little too much of my self-identity had been caught up in cricket. I discovered thoughts emerging from the back of my mind: "You're not special any more.

You're just like everyone else." I don't think I was arrogant as a young man, but cricket had, without my realizing it, become something of a crutch.

American swimmer and Olympic triathlete Barb Lindquist testifies to having struggled to find her significance in Christ, not from her race performances. While she knew in her head that in Christ she was loved and worthy, she didn't feel it in her heart. "After a few years of trying new athletic endeavours and failing," she says, "God broke me. Physically and mentally tired from trying to get my inner kudos from what I did, God revealed to me finally that He loved me regardless of my performance. If I ran 8 miles or none that day, if I weighed 150 pounds or 124 pounds, it didn't matter—His love was unconditional. What a freedom that was to know His love for me was not based on how I looked or raced. God brought stability to my life, despite the ups and downs of being an elite athlete."[9]

Conclusion

The experience of the American Christian swimmer Josh Davis is both illuminating and encouraging. Josh, like all athletes, has experienced the highs and the lows of his sport. Surprisingly for some, he experienced both at the 1996 Atlanta Olympics. There certainly were the highs, as he won three relay gold medals. He was the lead-off swimmer in the United States' 4 x 200 metres relay team, swimming a personal best in the final

---

9   Barb Lindquist, 'Search for Significance', in Davis, *The Goal and the Glory*, pp. 28-9 (quote from p. 29).

and leaving his team in first place when he handed over to the second swimmer. His teammates swam so well that Team USA won by over a body length. Says Josh: "The joy and relief we felt was indescribable".[10] Soon afterwards, there was the medal presentation, mutual congratulations, media interviews, and general adulation.

But the next morning, the adrenalin was gone. "Having had a taste of glory, I now felt empty", he says. "It was sobering to experience the shock of a high so high followed by a low so low." Josh turned to his Bible and read 1 Peter 1:7: "your faith [is] of greater worth than gold". He found comfort in knowing that his relationship with Jesus was more valuable than a gold medal.[11]

While Josh won three relay gold medals at the 1996 Olympics, an individual Olympic medal eluded him. Four years later, he was at the 2000 Olympic Games in Sydney. His best event was the 200 metres freestyle, and he qualified for the final. After 14 years and 30,000 miles of training, this was his big chance for an individual Olympic medal—perhaps gold. Davis was the American champion, but there were other superstars in the field including Australia's Ian Thorpe, Holland's Pieter van den Hoogenband, and Italy's Massimiliano Rosolino. Josh prayed before the event: "Lord, help me to go all out for you and with you, regardless of time or place. Thank you for being with me. Let's have some fun!"

---

10 Josh Davis, 'Fleeting Highs and Lasting Joys', in Davis, *The Goal and the Glory*, p. 148.
11 Davis, 'Fleeting Highs and Lasting Joys', pp. 148-50 (quote from p. 149).

The gun went and the race was on. Josh touched first at the 50-metre mark on world-record pace. At 100 metres, Josh, Ian and Pieter were neck-and-neck. At 150 metres, Ian and Pieter had slightly pulled away and were tied for first, with Josh just behind, and Massimiliano a metre back. Then, on the last lap, the Italian slowly caught Josh and touched fractionally ahead. Josh looked up and saw the number 4 next to his name. He had missed an individual medal by the barest of margins.

He recounts: "They say that 4th place is the worst place in the Olympics to be in because, whether you're last place or 4th place, neither of you receives a medal. But I looked at my time, and I saw that I had swam a 1:46.7! It broke my own American record by a good margin and would have easily won the previous Olympics. I realized that my prayer had been answered! God was with me during the race, so that I could swim my best, and He was with me now. God had been glorified, and I had swum faster than ever before. I was part of the greatest 200 metre freestyle race of all time."[12]

Despite this realization, Josh admits that he was overwhelmed with disappointment. Missing out on a medal by .07 of a second cut deep. He admits to having cried, but turned in the right direction. "I finally found comfort and strength by remembering the fact that God loves me unconditionally. [...] In our [i.e. America's] cultural economy, performance determines worth, but in God's economy, Christ's performance determines value."[13]

---

12 Josh Davis, 'Foreword', in Null, *Real Joy*, pp. vii-ix (quotes from pp. viii-ix).
13 Davis, 'Foreword', p. ix.

The joy of sport is best experienced when our relationship with God is strong.

SPORTSMANSHIP IN AN UNSPORTING WORLD

Sport and good character

**Whatever happens, conduct yourselves in a manner worthy of the gospel of Christ.
(Philippians 1:27)**

///

Brian Booth—for many his name is almost synonymous with sportsmanship in Australian cricketing circles. He was also a very good all-around athlete, representing Australia in both cricket and hockey. But it is for cricket that he is best known. A stylish batsman and sharp fieldsman, he played 29 test matches for his country in the 1960s, captaining the side on two occasions.

Brian became a Christian as a young man and, over the years, has given countless sermons and talks at Christian gatherings. But his faith has impacted his actions as well as his words. Back in his playing days, Brian's Christian faith influenced how he played the game and how he interacted with people, and it is illuminating to see how this has been viewed by others. In the 1970s, Australian cricket writer Ray Robinson penned a popular book entitled *On Top Down Under* about Australia's test cricket captains. The book contains a chapter about Brian Booth. Ray describes how Brian graciously accepted every umpiring decision, and was in the habit of 'walking' if he knew he had edged the ball and was out.[1] He continues:

> Loose shots had no more place in his career than loose living. He responded to countless requests to address church and youth rallies. [...] Amid coarse slang and ribaldry in the locker-rooms his quiet dignity contained no trace of a holier-than-thou attitude. He steadfastly tried to live up to scriptural tenets.[2]

The conclusion to the chapter reads:

> If a prize were offered for fairplaymanship among Australia's post-war cricketers Brian Booth ought to win hands down, not only for deserving it but because I feel other unblemished sportsmen would not accept nomination against him.[3]

These words are far from unique. Kerry O'Keeffe was an Australian cricketer in the 1970s, and is now a very colourful commentator and writer. When younger, Kerry played for the

---

1 For non-cricket lovers, 'walking' describes a batsman voluntarily leaving the playing arena, before the umpire has made a decision, when they know they are out. It is considered to be very good sportsmanship.
2 Ray Robinson, *On Top Down Under: Australia's Cricket Captains*, Cassell, Stanmore, 1975, p. 277.
3 Robinson, p. 279.

same local first grade club as Brian. In his quirky autobiography, *According to Skull*, Kerry writes:

> Batting at number three was Brian Booth, a wristy Test batsman who could whip the ball through midwicket with the same dexterity as VVS Laxman. He was a committed Baptist and his genuineness and sense of fair play were a shining example of how one could live one's life. His grace in both victory and defeat should have been more obvious to a somewhat headstrong young leg spinner [Kerry is referring to himself here]. Nonetheless, whenever I recall spending time with him on those Saturday afternoons, I am filled with the warmth of worthwhile reminiscence.[4]

In the 1990s, Brian wrote a booklet entitled *Sport and Sportsmanship* in which he promoted the view that "It's not whether you win or lose but how you win or lose".[5] He was very much aware of the pressures placed on people at the higher echelons of the game—pressures relating to money, violent play, drugs, sledging, and the need to win. These pressures filtered down and also affected sportspeople at lower levels, including youth. Brian was very concerned that people keep their sport in perspective and play in a competitive but sportsmanlike manner.

For almost two centuries, sport has been very strongly associated with good character. It has been seen as a place

---

4   Kerry O'Keeffe, *According to Skull: An Entertaining Stroll Through the Life of Kerry O'Keeffe*, ABC, Sydney, 2004, pp. 14-15.
5   Brian Booth, *Sport and Sportsmanship: A Christian perspective towards 2000*, Australian Christian Forum on Education, Lidcombe, Sydney, 1998.

where good character can be both *developed* and *displayed*. The term *sportsmanship* itself is a case in point. The word has been defined as "behaviour in sport that is fair and shows respect to the other players".[6] Thus, sportsmanship is a subset of good Christian character—the expression of certain Christian qualities in the sporting context.

Developing good character

God is very concerned that Christians develop and display good character. "Whatever happens," writes Paul, "conduct yourselves in a manner worthy of the gospel of Christ" (Phil 1:27). That is a big ask! How can anyone ever be sufficiently *worthy* of the gospel? Of course in one sense we can't—we'll never be perfect—but what the text is getting at is that we should strive to live up to the gospel. This will involve our seeking to become more and more like Christ in our words and actions. Colossians 3:12-14 sets out some of the things that this will entail:

> **Therefore, as God's chosen people, holy and dearly loved, clothe yourselves with compassion, kindness, humility, gentleness and patience. Bear with each other and forgive one another if any of you has a grievance against someone. Forgive as the Lord forgave you. And over all these virtues put on love, which binds them all together in perfect unity.**

These are noble goals, but how do we achieve them? And what role might sport have to play in the process? Thankfully, the

---

6 'Sportsmanship', *Cambridge Dictionary*: dictionary.cambridge.org/dictionary/english/sportsmanship.

Bible does not simply describe Christian character and leave it at that. Neither does it describe such character and then urge us to go out and play sport so as to achieve it. While God may use sport to help refine our character, it is not his primary way. Ultimately, we seek to develop our character in the same way that we work at any other aspect of our Christian life—*we* work at it, and *God* works in us. It really is like teamwork.

We read of this team arrangement in Colossians 1. Paul speaks of how he proclaims, admonishes and teaches with a view to presenting "everyone fully mature in Christ" (Col 1:28). How does he go about doing this? "To this end I strenuously contend with all the energy Christ so powerfully works in me" (Col 1:29). Paul strenuously contends—*he* does the work. At the very same time, Christ works powerfully in him. It is teamwork—Paul works hard with God's strength. It is the same with all areas of Christian living—we work, and God works in us.

This truth is seen in the testimony of former Australian rugby league representative Brad Mackay. While never a really dirty player, Brad admits to having been "a pretty dirty player" when he was young. But after becoming a Christian, things changed. "I decided not to play dirty anymore", he says. "In fact, I didn't even want to play dirty. The desire to do that had left me."[7] *Brad* resolved not to play dirty, and *God* seems to have taken away his former desire to play in that way. God seems to have used sport in this way to develop Brad's Christian character.

---

7   Ric Chapman and Ross Clifford, *The Gods of Sport: Sports Stars Converted to Greatness*, Albatross, Sutherland, 1995, p. 65.

SPORTSMANSHIP IN AN UNSPORTING WORLD

When it comes to developing good character, the Christian is called to take deliberate steps. Paul instructs believers to "put off your old self" (Eph 4:22) with all its negative character traits, and to "put on the new self" with all its positive character traits, the self that is "created to be like God in true righteousness and holiness" (Eph 4:24). This will involve conscious, deliberate thought and effort. For a start, it will involve reading the Bible so that we know what *is* and what *isn't* good character. We will also need to pray that God would change us and give us the desire to change.

Former Australian Rugby Union captain Nick Farr-Jones speaks of the importance of this practice in his life. "I look at my weaknesses", he says, "and pray about them so they will not be a stumbling block to myself or to anyone else". As well as confessing our shortcomings and asking God to change us, we can also pray that we would develop spiritual strength. The apostle Paul prays, for example, that the Philippian Christians would be "filled with the fruit of righteousness" (Phil 1:11). We could usefully pray the same for ourselves and others.

Are you aware of any character weaknesses when it comes to you and your sport? For example, are you overly aggressive? Do you cheat? Are you a poor loser? Are there positive character traits in which you would like to be stronger? Patience? Humility? Thoughtfulness?

We need to take action here. Fortunately, as noted, we are not fighting this battle alone. God is working in us. When Paul writes to the Christians at Colossae, he says that they "have put on the new self, *which is being renewed* in knowledge in the image of its Creator" (Col 3:10). God was bringing about decisive change in the Colossians' character—as he was (and is) with Brad and Nick, and as he will be with us as we follow him. What an encouragement this is!

Life in an unsporting world

Many like to think of sport as a place where good character might be developed—and it certainly can do this. Unfortunately, that is not always the case. In fact, the change often goes in the opposite direction. The sporting environment can sometimes be a destroyer rather than a developer of character.

Pete Nicholas, a former Oxford University rugby union representative and now a Church of England minister, testifies to the impact of sport in his pre-Christian life. "If anything, sport back then made me a more arrogant and proud person. I was harsh and dismissive of others, and self-righteous. I didn't like the man I was becoming." Perhaps you can think of people for whom sport seems to be doing their character more harm than good.

Why is it that sport—a good thing ultimately given to us by God—can function in this negative way? It is because, like all good things, it takes place in a fallen world with sinful people taking part. Both on and off the field, sportspeople—and those associated with them—can act in most unsportsmanlike ways. The pressure to win and the heightened emotions often associated with sport can cause people to lose their moral compass. To say that examples of poor behaviour abound is, sadly, an understatement. Bad actions and attitudes are found in abundance everywhere from the local park to the international arena.

On the field, there is verbal and physical abuse of players, referees and supporters. Physical abuse can involve punching, kicking, biting and spitting. There is cheating of every kind, from illegally impeding an opponent or diving, right through to ball tampering and match fixing.

Off the field, things are no better. We hear of sportspeople engaging in drunkenness, brawls, domestic violence and sexual assault. As I was writing this section, I looked at the sports section of an Australian news website. Of the six main stories, one involved a prominent sportsman who had admitted in court to assault and urinating in public during a night out. Journalist Simon Barnes wrote in *The Times* of London that, while professional athletes are required to set a moral example, it is a burden "for which they have no inclination and little aptitude".[8] His comment is perhaps a little overstated, but it's certainly true for many players. If we are relying on sport to provide our role models, we need to ask whether we are looking in the right place for life inspiration, and we need to think about what sort of example we are setting to others.

As we probably all know, these sorts of shortcomings are not limited to the rich and famous. They can also be found at more localized levels of sport. I spoke with some young adults at my church who are involved in cricket, soccer, rugby, netball and softball. They love playing their various sports, but

---

8   Simon Barnes, 'Athletes, the Naughty Vicars of the 21st Century', *The Times* (London), 23 September 2011, p. 93; cited in Watson and Parker, p. 28.

they also mentioned that they had encountered excessive drinking, bad language, a culture of bullying, the objectification of women, verbal and physical niggling, and poorly behaved parents. I could endorse this list—and add a few other things to it.

Disillusioned assessments of sporting culture are not hard to find. Two Australian academics, Douglas Booth (who formerly played Australian Rules football for St Kilda) and Colin Tatz, examined the Australian scene and concluded: "we find little to celebrate in the Australian sporting character, propped up as it is by pampered temperamental 'stars', uncharitable and biased journalists, unprincipled, unscrupulous and over-indulged officials, and increasingly obnoxious crowds".[9] American academic Shirl Hoffman asserts that there is not just a gap but a chasm between the Christian worldview and popular sports culture, which he sees as "narcissistic, materialistic, self-interested, violent, sensational, coarse, racist, sexist, brazen, raunchy, hedonistic, body-destroying, and militaristic".[10] We might want to argue about the extent to which these social commentators may or may not have overstated the problem, but there are underlying truths to which they point.

Not only is the world of sport damaged, but this damaged world can tempt those of us who take part to behave poorly. Let me illustrate with a personal example. I remember, as a teenager, bowling in a representative cricket game and dis-

---

9 Booth and Tatz, p. 210.
10 Hoffman, *Good Game*, p. 11.

missing one of the batsmen on the other team. I was a little frustrated that it had taken me so long to get him out, and within seconds I was pointing him towards the pavilion in a manner I'd seen displayed by an international cricketer of the era. I was a Christian, but was not behaving in a very sportsmanlike manner. One of the umpires, Tom Brooks, a former state cricketer and international umpire, stepped in immediately and indicated to me—and anyone else within earshot—in no uncertain terms that this was NOT the way to play the game. I have never forgotten it, and have since appreciated what he did.

Pointing to the damaged nature of the sporting world does not necessarily mean that we should avoid it. *Every* area of human life is damaged by sin. The thing to do is not necessarily to remove ourselves from these spheres of life, but to be aware of the dangers so that we can avoid them and live as a Christian within the world of sport.

Displaying good character

Kris Hogan was the coach of a high school American football team in Texas called the Grapevine Faith Christian Lions. The Lions became famous across America because of a 2008 game against the Gainesville State School Tornadoes. The Tornadoes were no ordinary side—their school was a maximum security correctional facility!

Most weeks, the Lions would win in front of hundreds of parents and schoolmates. They had good training facilities and their own home ground. By contrast, the Tornadoes had no home ground, almost no fans, and no wins that season. But at this game Kris Hogan organized for things to be a little different.

Before the game, many of his school's parents and students formed a 40-metre line cheering the Tornadoes players onto the field. Before kick-off, half the Lions' fans and cheerleaders moved to the Tornadoes' side of the stadium where they cheered, by name, for the stunned opposition players. Some were encouraging kids they didn't know to tackle their own sons. As it happened, the Lions won 33-14, but that did not really matter. After the game, both teams met together to pray. One of the Tornadoes players prayed, "Lord, I don't know how this happened, so I don't know how to say thank you, but I never would've known there were so many people in the world that cared about us."[11] Each member of the Tornadoes team received a bag with dinner and a devotional, and they left very different people to those they had been when they arrived.

The game was a transformative experience for the boys from Gainesville State School. The game also captured the imagination of the American public. As word spread, Kris appeared on ESPN, The 700 Club, and local television shows, along with doing dozens of radio and newspaper interviews. In the end, the NFL Commissioner invited Kris and his wife to attend the Super Bowl.[12]

Why did this game attract so much attention? Because, in a sporting world so often marked by egocentricity, violence and

---

11 David Thomas, *Remember Why You Play: Faith, Football, and a Season to Believe*, Tyndale, Carol Stream, 2010, pp. 231.
12 Thomas, pp. 212-40.

dishonesty, this game captured what so many would like to see sport achieve. It was sport at its very best.

Jesus said:

> "You are the salt of the earth. But if the salt loses its saltiness, how can it be made salty again? It is no longer good for anything, except to be thrown out and trampled underfoot.
>
> "You are the light of the world. A town built on a hill cannot be hidden. Neither do people light a lamp and put it under a bowl. Instead they put it on its stand, and it gives light to everyone in the house. In the same way, let your light shine before others, that they may see your good deeds and glorify your Father in heaven." (Matt 5:13-16)

The actions of Kris Hogan, his team, their parents, and the whole school were not only a fine example of good sportsmanship, but also a great example of what it means for Christians to be salt and light. We need to play sport in a Christlike way—which will usually mean doing our best, but will always mean competing in a sportsmanlike manner. It will often make us stand out in a sporting world which so often falls short of the sporting ideal.

Danger areas

Christians will often find themselves striving to display sportsmanship in the most unsporting of environments. The question is: Will we positively influence our environment, or will our environment negatively influence us? Let's briefly consider some of the danger areas.

Cheating

This can take many forms. There are a whole host of ways in which a person might deliberately break the rules in an effort to gain an unfair advantage. Often this is done in a way that they hope the referee or umpire will not notice—for example, illegally holding or impeding another player, ball tampering, or taking banned performance-enhancing drugs. There are also forms of cheating which are committed right out in the open, such as the professional foul—a deliberate act of illegal play committed with a view to gaining an advantage for one's team.[13] Whatever form it takes, the temptation to cheat often becomes stronger the more obsessed we are with winning.

An American physician named Bob Goldman carried out a survey that produced some disturbing results. He asked 198 athletes whether they would take a banned drug if they were guaranteed to win and not be caught. Out of the 198, 195 said that they would! The results then get even more troublesome. Goldman asked if they would take a performance-enhancing substance if they knew they would not be caught, win every event they entered in the next five years, and then die from

---

13 In some sports, it *might* be a little less clear that a deliberate foul should be referred to as 'cheating'. It has been put to me that in basketball, a deliberate foul is generally an accepted part of the game. For example, someone might foul another player on purpose (*knowing* they will get called for the foul) so that their opponent will have to shoot free throws rather than get an easy basket. Is that cheating? Should a Christian be discouraged from engaging in such behaviour? It would be good to discuss this sort of 'grey area' with mature Christians who are involved in your sport. Generally, I would suggest that the key thing is to play in a way that is in accordance with accepted practice, *and* is consistent with the spirit of the game.

the side effects. Over half said that they would! Would *you* ever think of answering 'yes' to one of those questions?[14]

Cheating is definitely not 'loving our neighbour' (Mark 12:31). It has a lot in common with lying in that it can involve harmful deception, and the Bible has much to say against lying: "The LORD detests lying lips, but he delights in people who are trustworthy" (Prov 12:22).[15]

Is cheating a danger for you? Make it your business to be someone who plays by the rules.

Selfish play

The player who hogs the ball and refuses to pass it; the player who plays for themselves and not for the team; the player who gets others to help them warm up but then refuses to help anyone else; the player whose every action indicates that, in their view, they are the centre of the universe—we all know them. But are we one of them? What would our fellow competitors and teammates say about us? Does our behaviour indicate that we think that other people matter, or does it reveal that we care only about ourselves?

Paul says: "Do nothing out of selfish ambition or vain conceit. Rather, in humility value others above yourselves, not looking to your own interests but each of you to the interests of the others" (Phil 2:3-4). Showing selfishness is an example of disobedience to God. In addition, selfish players are rarely popular players; by being selfish, we risk alienating our teammates.

---

14 Treat, p. 402.
15 See also Exod 20:16; Eph 4:25; Col 3:9.

Why might sportspeople be selfish? They may be obsessively ambitious, crave the attention of others, or simply be immature. If you realize you are being too self-focused, prayerfully consider why you may be like that, then take steps to deal with it. Why not resolve to compete in a way that shows that you think other people matter?

Verbal abuse

This can be a very challenging area. We all do things in the heat of the moment which we later regret. Perhaps we are playing a game and someone fouls us, or behaves in an arrogant way, or does something annoying, or plays very poorly, or plays very well, or is simply playing against us. If sufficiently provoked, we may lose our temper and verbally react. Verbal abuse may be directed towards other competitors, one's teammates, spectators, or an umpire. Who hasn't seen teams imploding, or disgruntled sportspeople mouthing off at referees?

I would expect that most Christian sportspeople will, on occasions, lose their tempers and say things they regret. This is true of believers in all sorts of contexts—for example, work, home, and even at church. Verbal abuse is clearly wrong: "But now you must also rid yourselves of all such things as these: anger, rage, malice, slander, and filthy language from your lips" (Col 3:8). If we fall into 'heat of the moment' verbal abuse, we must confess it to God, apologize to the relevant parties, and pray that God will change our hearts.

What about the Christian who is always losing their temper and 'mouthing off' when they play sport? If a believer is simply unable to play a particular sport without repeatedly losing their temper and resorting to verbal abuse, I would advise them to give up the sport—at least until their Christian maturity develops to a point where they can control themselves.

But it is not just the 'heat of the moment' stuff. Sometimes, a sportsperson will abuse another player for tactical reasons. The aim is to induce the opponent to lose their temper or their concentration. Christians should never employ premeditated verbal abuse.

What about verbal banter on the field? I have sometimes enjoyed a bit of good-natured verbal interchange when playing sport. But when does a bit of banter turn into verbal abuse? Context is important here. A bit of banter can be good fun, but verbal abuse is always wrong. At the end of the day, we should strive to conduct ourselves "in a manner worthy of the gospel of Christ" (Phil 1:27). Are we behaving in a way that shows love towards all involved? If, despite our best intentions, we make a mistake and say something that we later regret, it is always possible to confess it to God and apologize to those involved.

Physical abuse

This is another challenging area. Children will sometimes lose their temper and resort to hitting another person in anger or frustration. Parents work hard to train them out of this sort of behaviour as soon as they possibly can. But resorting to physical abuse is a very, very, very serious problem when it is still being displayed by adults.

Perhaps the only place where physical abuse by adults is given any sort of social acceptability—wrongly, I hasten to add—is on the sports field. For example, some rugby fans might think that a good punch-up can 'bring a game to life', or that a few punches in the scrum are simply 'part of the game'. But physical abuse of any sort, on or off the field, is always wrong.

We are not talking about hard physical play. Depending on the sport, age group and context, it can be quite appropriate to play (within the rules) in a physically hard manner. With people who are appropriately matched and prepared, and consent to take part, it is quite in order for a Christian to dish out a hard tackle in a game of rugby or to bowl a bouncer in a game of cricket (especially now that batsmen have appropriate protective equipment).

What we are talking about here is illegal physical play. This may be a 'heat of the moment' action—for example, pushing or punching someone after a heavy collision in a netball game. It may also be planned and premeditated—for example, deliberately throwing a few punches at an opponent to put them off their game. We also need to beware of legal physical play that is fuelled by anger or hatred, which is always wrong for the Christian. For example, it would be possible to tackle an opponent on the soccer field in a legal but hate-filled way.

The writer of Proverbs says: "Do not envy the violent or choose any of their ways" (Prov 3:31). Paul writes that the "acts of the flesh" include things like "hatred" and "fits of rage" (Gal 5:19-20), and, as we saw above, insists that we must rid ourselves of a list of things that includes anger and rage (Col 3:8), which so often lead to physical abuse on the sporting field. We should never agree to take part in premeditated physical abuse on the sporting field. We must also work to eliminate acts of physical abuse caused by a loss of temper. If we *do* lose our temper and engage in physical abuse, as with verbal abuse, we must confess it to God, apologize to the relevant parties, and pray that God will change our heart.

I expect that many Christians will fall down in this area from time to time. But what of the Christian who is *always* losing their temper and engaging in physical abuse? Again, as with verbal abuse, if they are simply unable to play a particular sport without repeatedly resorting to physical violence, I would advise them to give up the sport until they have developed self-control.

Spitting the dummy

This term is used to describe the situation where a person behaves poorly when things don't go their way. I deliberately use the term as it captures the childish nature of the reaction. I expect we have all seen examples of dummy spitting. The opposition scores, and one of your players starts blaming you and all your teammates. An athlete is beaten in a race and storms off without speaking to anyone. A cricketer throws their bat in the dressing room after being dismissed. The coach of a losing side angrily blames the referee for the loss. Again, spitting the dummy does not bring God any glory and, for what it's worth, makes us look silly and childish.

Conclusion

As Christian athletes, we should seek to display godly character in every area of our athletic existence. This will include showing good sportsmanship. As we do this, God will use the process to further develop our character. The key is to work on our relationship with God, then to prayerfully seek to live out our faith both on and off the field. Why not resolve to make your name synonymous with good sportsmanship? For inspiration, perhaps you could read a biography of someone like Eric Liddell or Brian Booth. What a privilege to honour our Lord and Saviour in the heat of sporting battle, and what a great opportunity we have to bear witness to the transforming power of the gospel in the way we conduct our sporting lives.

We've already spoken of Linvoy Primus, the former Portsmouth FC defender. Converted during his time at the club, he was soon attending church, meeting with the club chaplain, and enjoying fellowship with a few Christian teammates. He learned that his identity was ultimately in Christ, not in being a good footballer. The chaplain encouraged him to see his footballing skill as a gift from God that he could use for God's glory. Linvoy sought to live out his faith both on and off the pitch. On the field, he sought to play in a godly way. Off the field, he took opportunities to serve his community in various ways. The London-based sports radio station talkSPORT was sufficiently impressed by Linvoy to pronounce him "Officially the nicest footballer in the world". A 2015 post on their website read as follows:

> Defender, charity worker, legend—Is anyone nicer than Linvoy Primus?
> That's the question Max Rushden and Barry Glendenning have asked a host [of] current and former professional footballers over the months on talkSPORT.

The general consensus—No.

The Warm Up duo even go as far as saying they are singlehandedly responsible for the Portsmouth hero's soon-to-be awarded MBE (where he will meet the Queen, who may be the only person to come close to rivalling Linvoy's niceness).[16]

Linvoy—who would be the first to admit that he is far from perfect and that any glory should go to God—strives, with God's help, to display sportsmanship in an often-unsporting world. And the world has taken notice.

---

16 'Officially the nicest footballer in the world—The Warm Up's Linvoy Primus Special', *talkSPORT*, 12 January 2015: talksport.com/football/231978/officially-nicest-footballer-world-warm-ups-linvoy-primus-special-150112132016/.

THE SPORTS FIELD AS MISSION FIELD

Sport and outreach

> When he saw the crowds, he had compassion on them, because they were harassed and helpless, like sheep without a shepherd. Then he said to his disciples, "The harvest is plentiful but the workers are few. Ask the Lord of the harvest, therefore, to send out workers into his harvest field."
> (Matthew 9:36-38)

///

It was hockey heaven, and Jill Ireland was living the dream. A fresher at Loughborough University, she was already playing in the university firsts. But not only that; her hero Mary Nevill, the former Great Britain hockey captain and Olympic bronze medallist, was her hockey coach, her personal tutor, and her lecturer in sports physiology. Playing hockey most days and enjoying the freedoms of campus life—for a sports-mad girl from Yorkshire, things could not have been much better.

Meanwhile, Lynda Hewitt, a final year student from Northern Ireland, was also in the university first team. An extremely fit and fiercely competitive player, she was also kind, funny, considerate and caring. "My first impressions of Lynda were mixed", admits Jill. "I couldn't work out what to think of her. She was a Christian. She didn't get drunk or go off with guys like some of the other girls in the team, so I didn't really know if that made her boring or, as I didn't really want to do those things anyway, whether she was someone to admire."

One day, Jill was boarding the team bus after a game for a three-hour journey back to Loughborough when she saw a seat free next to Lynda. Jill sat next to Lynda and the two girls started to chat. Before long, the conversation turned to boys! Jill asked Lynda if she had a boyfriend. Lynda said she did—a guy called Brian. They'd met at the university's Christian Union. This put Jill a little on edge, wondering if she was going to get Bible-bashed for a few hours.

To Jill's great surprise, Lynda said she'd prayed before going out with Brian. "What?" said Jill, suddenly interested. "You prayed about your boyfriend?" Up until then, Jill had thought of God as being some sort of distant, far off, Father Christmas type figure—not the sort of being you'd consult on something like boyfriends.

As the conversation moved on, Lynda talked about her relationship with God through Jesus. She explained that she talked to God through prayer; and that she knew God in the person of Jesus. She explained who Jesus was; why he came to earth, died on the cross, and rose from the dead; and how that affected her life. She told Jill that this was all an expression of God's unconditional love for people, despite their having turned away from him.

"I could see that Lynda was totally convinced Jesus was real, that he was alive and living, and that she knew him and had a relationship with him." Lynda spoke of how Jesus sustained her, led her and comforted her. Jill wanted to know more about this Jesus. Lynda offered to read the Bible with her, and they began meeting together to do this each week. Lynda gave Jill a copy of John's Gospel, answered questions, and introduced her to other Christians—including Christians who played sport. Jill found that the Bible was a book like no other, and that it penetrated her heart. Before long, she prayed to commit her life to Christ.

Lynda continued to read the Bible with her and took her to church. Jill started attending both the Christian Union and a Christians in Sport prayer group. The two girls helped run a Christian camp in Northern Ireland, and went on a Christians in Sport hockey mission trip to Kenya.

At the end of her studies, Jill's greatest desire was to work with Christians in Sport, and she was thrilled to be offered a job as their National Student Coordinator, a position that required her to move to Oxford. The job involved encouraging students in universities to do what Lynda had done for her— pray for their non-Christian teammates, play sport in a way that honoured God, and say something about Jesus when the opportunity arose.

In Oxford, Jill joined a local hockey club. "I was certainly keen to share my faith, and as soon as I joined the club I was praying specifically for some of my teammates by name." People soon found out that Jill was a Christian—questions about her job tended to give it away. After training on the first night, she found herself in a conversation with a teammate called Wendy, who arranged to drive Jill to a game so that she could talk to her about Christianity. As it turned out, Wendy had a friend named Simon, a Christian who had made it clear that he could not pursue a relationship with a woman who was not a believer. As such, Wendy had a lot of questions.

Jill and Wendy soon became friends and chatted for hours about all sorts of things, including the Christian faith. Jill invited her new friend to come to church with her, and the two of them began to read the Bible together. Soon, Wendy committed her life to Christ; she married Simon, and Jill became godmother to their two children. Over the next few years, Jill saw two other hockey teammates come to follow Jesus. "There is no greater privilege", she says, "than seeing God at work in a friend's life as he draws them to himself and they accept his wonderful offer of life in all its fullness!"

Friendship and faith

One of the main reasons people give for playing sport is to meet people and to form friendships. Some of the best things in my life have been the friendships I've made through sport. When our sports friends are Christians, there is the opportunity to encourage them in their faith—something we will consider in the next chapter. When they are not believers, there is the opportunity to be a Christian witness and to point them toward Christ—the focus of this chapter.

Sport can put Christians in contact with many people who would never think of darkening the door of a church or picking up a Bible. This presents us with both opportunities and dangers. As such, sport can be both a *mission field* and a *mine-*

field. The key to making it the former rather than the latter is to maintain and grow in our relationship with God.

Sport as a mission field

It is worth taking the time to reflect on the teammates, opponents, fellow competitors, coaches, administrators, umpires, and supporters with whom we rub shoulders. How do we view them? We know how Jesus saw those with whom he came into contact:

> When he saw the crowds, he had compassion on them, because they were harassed and helpless, like sheep without a shepherd. Then he said to his disciples, "The harvest is plentiful but the workers are few. Ask the Lord of the harvest, therefore, to send out workers into his harvest field." (Matt 9:36-38)

Jesus saw the world around him as a harvest field full of people in need of the gospel. He had compassion on them. He urged prayer for workers to go into the harvest fields.

Whether we realize it or not, whenever we play or watch sport with people who aren't Christians, we are in a mission field. To take advantage of the opportunities this provides, there are a number of things we can usefully do.

Remember you are an ambassador for Christ

We can spend many hours each week with others in a sporting context—games like cricket and golf can often take up most of a day. Whenever we spend time with people who don't yet know Christ as Lord, we are his representative. As Paul writes:

> We are therefore Christ's ambassadors, as though God were making his appeal through us. We implore you on Christ's behalf: Be reconciled to God. (2 Cor 5:20)

As the stories of Lynda and Jill above showed, sport gives us the opportunity to point people towards Christ, to share our faith, and to urge them to be reconciled to God.

The ex-rugby-playing Church of England minister Pete Nicholas came to faith through sporting contacts. He argues that some of the best evangelistic opportunities come through sport. "It can be easier there than in the workplace", he says. "At work you are supposed to be working, and there is often the associated pressure and stress. Furthermore, there is the thought that if a conversation goes badly you still have to work with that person. By contrast, social sport is a more relaxed environment. You are there as part of your leisure time. You spend regular time with these people, but you don't have to work next to them each day." (Of course, for the professional sportsperson, sport is more like a work environment—a place where we are also to be ambassadors for Christ.)

Some people who have been followers of Jesus for a long period of time end up with a lot of Christian friends, but no non-believing friends. If this is true for you, you may need to seek out people among whom you can be a Christian example. Playing a sport can be a great option. Regular sport gives us the opportunity to get to know others, and those with whom we compete have the chance to observe our lifestyle over an extended period. If they are open to discussing spiritual issues, we may be just the person with whom they will feel comfortable doing so.

Andrew Wingfield Digby, another Church of England minister and founding director of Christians in Sport in the UK, returned to playing seniors' cricket after several years away from the game. Besides helping him to keep fit and have fun, it keeps him in contact with non-believers. "The longer you serve in the church," he says, "the more time you spend with Christians. While there are many positives about this, I fear becoming a 'church functionary' who has lost contact with the non-Christian world. Sport enables me to meet and spend regular time with non-Christian men." I participate in seniors' athletics for similar fitness, fun, friendship and outreach opportunities. And I know many other Christians who take part in sport for similar reasons.

Know what you believe and why you believe it

If the people with whom we play (or watch) sport like or respect us, and if they know that we are Christians, there is every chance that we will end up in spiritual discussions with them. A teammate might ask us about our beliefs or about what we think on a particular issue. Even if we initiate the conversation, there is a good chance that they will be open to listening to some of what we have to say.

There are two things to consider here. If a sporting colleague asks us, "So what exactly is this stuff you believe in?", or "How in this day and age can you believe in something as unbelievable (or out-of-date or narrow-minded) as Christianity?", would we know what to say?

For some Christians, the thought of being asked such questions is a nightmare scenario—somewhat akin to being thrown into a ring with Mike Tyson. Yet it needn't be like this. The apostle Peter gives us some very helpful instruction on this point:

> **But in your hearts revere Christ as Lord. Always be prepared to give an answer to everyone who asks you to give the reason for the hope that you have. But do this with gentleness and respect. (1 Pet 3:15)**

Peter urges us to "be prepared" to talk about our faith—about *what* we believe and *why* we believe it. We prepare ourselves for a sports event by going to training or getting coached. So, too, we should prepare ourselves to speak about our Christian faith.

One of the best things we can do as Christians, whether or not we play sport, is to learn how to explain the good news (or 'gospel') about Jesus. Many Christians recognize the gospel when they hear it, but struggle to reproduce it themselves when given the opportunity. The problem is that most Christians who recognize the gospel think that they *can* reproduce it—but *recognition* and *reproduction* are two different skills. You might like to try this quick test: Without doing any preparation, grab a pen and paper and give yourself two minutes to write down a summary of the gospel. Then, get hold of a gospel outline—for example, from a gospel tract or booklet—and see how you have gone.

For the good of your sporting friends—to say nothing of your family, other friends, and work or study colleagues—

could I urge you to learn a gospel outline if you haven't done so already? Knowing *what* to say when we get the opportunity is just so helpful. It helps the person to whom we are speaking, and it takes a lot of the stress out of the situation for us. I am sure that both Jill and Wendy were very appreciative that when Lynda and Jill respectively shared the gospel with them, they knew what to say. And I'm sure Lynda and Jill were glad they were prepared, too!

There are many good resources that can help us to learn how to effectively communicate the gospel.[1] If you think you would struggle explaining the good news to someone, why not make it a project to learn how to do so in the next month?

It can also be helpful to consider how we would answer some of the big questions people may ask about our faith. While they may not be expressed in these exact terms, common questions often run along the following lines: Isn't Christianity a myth? Hasn't science disproved Christianity? What about all the suffering in the world? Do I have to give up drinking/sex/fun/sport to be a Christian? Isn't Christianity narrow-minded—for example, isn't it anti-women, anti-gay, or anti-other religions? How can you take Jesus' resurrection

---

[1] One of the best gospel outlines is *Two Ways to Live: The choice we all face* (Matthias Media, 2003). The outline and various resources are available at twowaystolive.com. Other very good outlines include *The Bridge to Life*, available at navlink.org/bridge; and Scripture Union Australia's *How to Know God* (1997). Good books on sharing the Christian faith with others include John Chapman, *Know and Tell the Gospel* (5th edn, Matthias Media, 2020); Sam Chan, *Evangelism in a Skeptical World: How to make the Unbelievable news about Jesus more Believable* (Zondervan, 2018); and Randy Newman, *Questioning Evangelism* (Kregel, 2004).

and miracles seriously? How can God send people to hell?

I became a follower of Jesus when I was about ten, but in late high school a lot of these sorts of questions started to occur to me. I talked to people from church, read books, and discovered answers that satisfied me. I found this process very helpful. I *loved* being a Christian, but the more I investigated, the more I realized there were very good *reasons* to believe. In fact, so good were these reasons that I considered it far more logical to believe than not to believe. Having worked through these issues has proved to be very helpful for me when speaking about my faith in the sporting world. Again, there are many good resources available if you want to prepare yourself in this area.[2]

Live and play Christianly

Of course, we must not only talk the talk; we must also walk the walk. Our lifestyle on and off the field should be consistent with the Christian message. None of us are perfect, but seeking to display Christian character (of the sort described in chapters 3 and 5) will prompt people to ask questions and to take seriously our answers.

In 1984, the Cambridge United Football Club signed Alan Comfort, a left-winger, from Queens Park Rangers. This meant that the writing was on the wall for Cambridge's left winger at the time—Graham Daniels. Not surprisingly, as

---

[2] Good books include Tim Keller, *The Reason for God* (Riverhead, 2008); Paul Little, *Know Why You Believe* (IVP, 2008); and John Dickson, *The Christ Files* (Zondervan, 2010).

Alan settled into his new club, he was a little wary of Graham, wondering how he would react given that Alan had taken his spot on the team. But as time progressed, Alan noticed something that surprised him:

> There was something different about him [Graham] that I couldn't quite understand. His contract was up, his wife was expecting their first child, he was out of the team. Nothing seemed to be going right for him, yet there was something special about him I couldn't really understand. He had something that I didn't have. In contrast, I had everything that I wanted. I had signed a really good contract, I was in the team, I thought I had made it, and yet I felt really empty. I thought it was material things that made you happy in life and I had them. He didn't and yet he had a happiness that I didn't. I had never seen anyone with so much security. He knew exactly where he was going. I watched him from a distance, trying to work it all out in my own mind, exactly what was going on. In the end I decided I had to find out for myself. I started talking to him and eventually I plucked up the courage to go to church with him.[3]

It has to be said that Graham did find it very hard to lose his spot in the team's starting line-up, but with God's help and the support of other Christians, he did his best to play and live in a godly way. In the end, Alan became a Christian believer.

Lest we think that these truths apply only to adults, consider the example of a young teenage boy called Damien. Growing up on the north coast of New South Wales, Damien enjoyed playing rugby league. Now an adult, he and his wife

---

3   Weir, p. 109.

attend my church. His wife told me that a few years back, she and her husband caught up with one of Damien's old childhood sporting friends named Jason. At the time they reconnected, Jason was studying to become a Presbyterian minister. Jason told them that Damien's positive example as a 13- or 14-year-old had really made an impression on him. Damien didn't swear or fight—in fact, his behaviour on and off the field stood out as being different. Jason knew that Damien was a Christian, and Damien's distinctive behaviour was one of the key reasons that Jason decided to investigate Christianity.

Like so many other Christian sportspeople, Graham and Damien were salt and light (Matt 5:13-14). Their lifestyles spoke of the difference that following Jesus made, and it changed their friends' lives.

Pray

As with every part of the Christian life, evangelism is a spiritual battle, and prayer is one of our chief weapons. Even the great apostle Paul sought the prayer support of others for his evangelistic ministry (Eph 6:19-20). Writing to the Colossians, he urges:

> Devote yourselves to prayer, being watchful and thankful. And pray for us, too, that God may open a door for our message, so that we may proclaim the mystery of Christ, for which I am in chains. Pray that I may proclaim it clearly, as I should. (Col 4:2-4)

If Paul valued prayer, how much more should we? In the same way that a sporting team won't go into a big game and leave one of their stars on the bench, neither should we leave prayer on the bench. We should pray that God would help us to live as Christians in the sporting environment, that he would give us opportunities to speak about Jesus, and that God's Spirit would open the hearts of our sporting friends and bring them to faith.

Trevor Goddard was one of the great South African cricketers of the last century, an all-rounder who opened the batting, bowled medium pace, and captained the team during the 1960s. Upon becoming a Christian, prayer became very important to him:

> After giving my heart to Jesus Christ in 1970, I realized that some of my old team mates thought I had gone crazy. Peter [Pollock, the great South African fast bowler], I am sure, thought I had gone all religious and funny! The result was that I was given a wide berth. I was a chap to steer clear of—and so Peter and I had very little contact.
>
> For my part, I listed the players I had played with, especially the team that went to Australia. I used to pray for them, going down the list praying for each one in turn, eventually coming to Peter Pollock and thinking: "Phew, Lord! You really have got a tough one here. I don't know how you will ever get him into the kingdom of God."
>
> Praise God, nothing is impossible for our Lord. Peter was the first to give his life to Christ and now serves God with the same enthusiasm as he bowled on his first tour of Australia—everything flat out and then a little extra, and I know he does it all to God's glory.[4]

---

4 From Peter Pollock, *Clean Bowled*; cited in Chapman and Clifford, pp. 20-1.

Make use of the time and opportunities

Mission takes time. People engaged in overseas cross-cultural ministry spend long periods—usually many years, in fact—learning a new language and culture, then winning the confidence and respect of those with whom they interact, before having the opportunity to effectively share their faith. While in most sporting contexts we already share the same language and culture, it will usually take time to win enough confidence and respect from those with whom we play that they will be ready to speak with us about personal and spiritual matters. Many sports require a weekly commitment, which gives us the time we need. We simply have to use that time well. "Be wise in the way you act toward outsiders; make the most of every opportunity" (Col 4:5).

Sometimes, opportunities present themselves in an obvious way. On one occasion, a sports friend who was going through a hard time came to me and said, "Liggo, what's it all about?" That was pretty direct. On another occasion, near the end of a night out with some sporting colleagues, a woman said to me: "Stephen, does it bother you that the other guys hassle you about being a Christian?" With that particular team there was often animated banter about my faith and what that meant I would and wouldn't do. It was all good fun, and I often dished out as good as I got. So I explained to her that the banter was all good-natured, and that I felt sorry that my teammates were *not* Christians. The conversation flowed on from there.

Sometimes, people's circumstances give us the opportunity to be proactive. If a teammate or a loved one of a teammate is sick, there are very few people who wouldn't appreciate our saying that we would pray for them. (Of course, we then have to do what we say!) Sometimes, the tragedy of sickness presents other opportunities. A poignant example features two great West Indian fast bowlers—Wes Hall, who played in the 1960s, and Malcolm Marshall, who played in the 1980s. In 1999, Malcolm, aged 41, was diagnosed with cancer of the colon. Wes, a Christian, takes up the story: "He was in trouble and I was fortunate enough to go to him and I said to him, 'Has anybody talked to you about your salvation?' He says, 'No'. I said, 'Well, I'm that man'." Wes spoke to him and told him that it was time to repent. Says Wes, "I thank God he did that".

But opportunities for sharing our faith won't always fall into our lap. Sometimes we will need to be bold and creative in getting our sporting colleagues to think about spiritual matters. As an example, carrying my Bible in my cricket kit bag was an attempt to do this.

Get people in contact with the gospel

As Paul says in Romans, "how can they believe in the one of whom they have not heard?" (Rom 10:14). It is a good point! One of the best things we can do for someone is to get them into contact with the gospel of Jesus Christ. We can do this in a variety of ways. As we have been discussing, we can explain it ourselves using a gospel outline. Another very helpful practice is to invite a person to read the Bible with you, as Jill did with Wendy. Initially, it might be best to go through one of the Gospels or one of Paul's shorter letters, such as Colossians. We might give someone a Bible, a Christian book, or the biography of a Christian sportsperson, which they can read on their own.

Christian videos and podcasts can also be helpful.

We could also invite people to an event at which they will hear something about the Christian faith—particularly about the good news of Jesus. You might be surprised at how many people will accept an invitation to church if the offer is made, particularly at times likes Christmas and Easter. Never underestimate the power of inviting someone. Even if they say 'no', don't view it as a failure. In my view, simply issuing an invitation is a victory—the other person has still been made to think about Christianity at some level.

In the early 1880s, the English cricketer CT Studd invited several of the English team to hear the great American evangelist Dwight L Moody. Two members of the team to accept the invitation were Ivo Bligh and Alan Steel. According to Studd's biographer, "Years later Bligh wrote and told CT how he daily prayed for him, and that he was trusting the Saviour; likewise Alan Steel".[5] While many secular sportspeople today may not instinctively warm to the idea of listening to a 'standard' Christian speaker, they might be open to hearing a Christian sportsperson. I have often found friends are quite willing—in fact, often very keen—to come and listen to Christian sportspeople.

Another option is to organize a *Christianity Explained* course, which I have done on a few occasions—either by myself, or with a Christian teammate (when there has been one). *Christianity Explained* is a non-denominational course that explains the gospel in a relaxed format over a number of

---

5   Grubb, p. 34.

weeks.[6] I first ran this course with my football team when I was in my early 20s. The left back and I sent everyone an invitation in the mail. Were we nervous? Yes. Did we pray? Certainly! How did our teammates react? With everything from interest, to mild amusement, to feeling a little awkward. Did it make anyone dislike us? No. Did anyone attend? Yes, about three or four guys plus one guy's girlfriend.

Since then, I have run *Christianity Explained* at two different cricket clubs. In each case, people attended and heard the gospel clearly explained. At no time did inviting people attract genuine hostility. In fact, looking back, a lot of guys probably thought it was very surprising; sure, some may have thought it was a little extreme, but I think most people probably figured that I was a Christian and so, naturally, I would want people to think about it.

As another example, Elizabeth Chambers told me that she and a Christian teammate organized a 'question night' for members of her hockey club. About nine women came along, and Elizabeth and her friend did their best to answer the questions that their friends posed about the Christian faith. At the end of the evening, Elizabeth asked if anyone wanted to meet up to read the Bible with her; one girl said yes.

With a bit of prayerful imagination, there are many things we can organize to introduce our friends to Jesus.

---

6   See christianityexplained.com for full details.

Share your story

Simply telling others of what God has done in our lives is another particularly powerful option. People today are very interested in stories; they are also drawn to practical things that actually work. A Christian testimony combines both. It might be the account of how we first became followers of Jesus. It might be the account of how God helped us to deal with particular circumstances in life, which may include sharing how God helped us in the face of injury, in the ups and downs of our sporting existence, or in our lives generally. Not only do people find personal stories engaging; it also means we are speaking about a subject on which we are the world expert: God's impact on our lives.

There are a number of testimonies described in the New Testament—for example, check out the effect of the story of the man born blind who was healed by Jesus in John 9, or the story of Paul's conversion in Acts 26.

Work as a team

Many of us enjoy team sports in which we work together with others for a common cause. The Christian church is also a team whose members are working together for a common cause—in our case, making disciples of all nations (Matt 28:18-20). Here are a few ways in which we can work as a team:

- » Ask our church, Bible study group or Christian friends to pray for our sports outreach. I know of one minister who asked this of his church when he was chaplain at a rugby league club.

- » If you find a Christian teammate, organize an evangelistic event together. I found it easier to run *Christianity Explained* when I was doing it with a fellow club member.
- » Organize occasions where we get some Christian sports-playing friends together with some non-Christian sports-playing friends. For example, a friend of mine once organized an Oztag team in which half were believers and half non-believers.
- » Similarly, churches can organize sports events or competitions that mix Christians and non-Christians.
- » If you are going to join a local sporting team, why not grab one or two Christian friends and have them join with you?

Consider public speaking opportunities

Sometimes, when sporting achievements are of sufficient interest to the general public, we might find ourselves being invited by a church or Christian group to speak about our sport and our faith. Many of the more well-known sportspeople mentioned in this book have received such invitations. If you find yourself in a position to take up such an opportunity, start by talking to a wise, trusted Christian about whether they think it is a good thing for you to do. If you decide to proceed, pray for your preparation and for the event. It can be a good idea to ask a trusted Christian leader to look over what you plan to say. Then, as appropriate to the circumstances, do your best to point people to Jesus.

Persist

Now in his fifties, Rico Tice's days of playing rugby union with Bristol and Oxford Universities are long gone. He is married with children and serves as a minister at a large central London church. "I'm now time poor", he tells me, "and unable to play the amount of sport that I did when I was younger. But I do, from time to time, get together with my old rugby friends for dinners, drinks or games of golf. And here's the thing—we often have good spiritual discussions. You see, we're all older, we're no longer competing with each other anymore, we've all been through the ups and downs of life together, and they've watched me over the years. They know I really believe what I preach and, as a result, are more inclined to listen to me than when we were in our twenties."

Rico showed me his prayer list. Prominent on it were the names of about 40 men with whom he once played rugby. For Rico, seeing the sports field as a mission field involves persistence and prayer. For us, too, our prayer for and contact with our sporting friends can continue long after our playing days are finished.

Expect that some will be interested… and some won't

Time for a reality check: How do you think our efforts at sports outreach will go? What do you think we should expect to achieve? The most likely outcome is that some will be interested in the gospel of Jesus Christ, and some won't. This has certainly been my experience, and I am in very good company. Jesus found that many were interested in listening to his message (e.g. Mark 2:1-2), while many were not (e.g. Mark 6:1-6). The apostle Peter found the same thing (e.g. Acts 2:14-41; Acts 4:1-22). In each case—Jesus', Peter's, and mine—it would be fair to say that more people fell into the *not really interested* category.

While it is incredibly encouraging when we see people coming to Christ and being saved, it is a cause of real grief that most people are not interested. It might be helpful at this point to identify our responsibility and God's. It is our responsibility to promote the gospel, which includes being prepared to give an account of what it is that we believe. But we are *not* responsible for people's responses. That is between them and God. We can't *make* someone a Christian. Our job is to prepare ourselves, and to prayerfully and wisely do what we can.

Remember that God is with you

Near the beginning of Romans, Paul writes: "For I am not ashamed of the gospel, because it is the power of God that brings salvation to everyone who believes: first to the Jew, then to the Gentile" (Rom 1:16). Why do you think that Paul said that he was "not ashamed" of the gospel? I suspect one reason was that so many people *are* tempted to be ashamed of it. The message about Jesus can sometimes seem distant, or irrelevant, or unbelievable, or foolish. We may suspect that people will be bored, or patronizing, or angry if we mention it. As a result, we often shy away from presenting or promoting the gospel to others. I have missed countless opportunities to speak of Jesus over the years because of nervousness or fear—both in the sports world and elsewhere. I suspect most Christians reading this book could say the same thing.

In the light of this, we need to remember two greatly encouraging truths. First, God is a God of grace. We are forgiven for all our sins, including our many sins of omission. We can confess our failings to God, knowing that he loves us and—thanks to Jesus' death on the cross—has forgiven us. Second, we can take great comfort from Jesus' last words in the Gospel of Matthew. After commissioning his followers to "go and make disciples of all nations" (Matt 28:19), he reassures them with the following promise: "And surely I am with you always, to the very end of the age" (Matt 28:20). Whether we find ourselves speaking or standing up for Christ on the field, in the dressing room, or at a club, pub or nightclub, Jesus is with us!

Sport as a minefield

As we have said throughout this book, for all the opportunities that sport provides for friendship and for Christian witness, there are also genuine dangers. Like so many other areas of life, sport can be a minefield for the believer. We have already discussed in earlier chapters many of the common dangers. These challenges can be all the greater when we are one of the few Christians (and perhaps the only one) in our particular sporting context. We need to take these dangers seriously. As always, the key is to work on maintaining our relationship with God through Bible reading, prayer and consistent Christian fellowship.

The fact that sport can expose us to these dangers does not necessarily mean that we should withdraw from the sporting world. Rather, we should seek to fight the good fight within it (1 Tim 6:12). Jesus speaks of this 'in the world but not of the world' idea in his prayer for his disciples in John 17:

> "I have given them your word and the world has hated them, for they are not of the world any more than I am of the world. My prayer is not that you take them out of the world but that you protect them from the evil one. They are not of the world, even as I am not of it. Sanctify them by the truth; your word is truth. As you sent me into the world, I have sent them into the world." (John 17:14-18)

Fighting the good fight in the world is not easy. We will all fail, stumble and slip up. I certainly do. At times like this it is helpful to remember that we are saved by grace: "For it is by grace you have been saved, through faith—and this is not from yourselves, it is the gift of God—not by works, so that no one can boast" (Eph 2:8-9). In addition, it is reassuring to know that Jesus sympathizes with us in our weaknesses: "For we do not have a high priest who is unable to empathize with our weaknesses," says the writer of Hebrews, "but we have one who has been tempted in every way, just as we are—yet he did not sin" (Heb 4:15).

But what if, through spending time with non-believers, we find ourselves consistently failing in some area? What if we are simply unable to maintain our sporting involvement without lapsing into idolatrous attitudes or drunkenness or sexual immorality? In this case, we will either need to give up that sport, or give up playing that sport with those people. It may be that our Christian maturity will one day develop to a point where we can return to that context and stand firm in our faith. It may be that it will not. As enjoyable and important as our sport may be, our relationship with God is far more important!

Conclusion

In the early 1990s, Graham Crew became chaplain to the St George Rugby League team in Australia. "It was great for me as a local pastor", he says. "It got me out from the church environment and gave me the opportunity to rub shoulders with a lot of non-Christian men. It was also good for my church as I organized for church members to pray for the players and officials at the club."

Brad Mackay was one of the younger St George players at the time. Although already a New South Wales and Australian representative, Brad describes himself as having "lived a pretty normal young bloke's lifestyle". He met a girl called Joanne, whom he liked, and they started dating. But Joanne was a Christian, and during the relationship she decided that she needed to get her Christian life back on track.

Joanne challenged Brad by saying that, because she was a Christian and he wasn't, she couldn't marry him. Somewhat surprised, Brad said that he believed in God and that she shouldn't stress out about it. But, in reality, he realized that he knew next to nothing about God or Christianity, and that he had better do something to rectify this.

Having heard that there was a chaplain at the club, Brad decided to contact him. He rang Graham and asked whether he could come and see him and perhaps even come along to his church. Graham, of course, said yes. So Brad started attending Graham's church and meeting with him regularly. The two men talked a lot and read the Bible, and Graham answered Brad's questions. To his great surprise, Brad felt better after going to church. "It made me feel clean", he says. "It was like a shower for the soul."

After a few months, Graham said to Brad that he had told him all he could. Brad said that he was not going to become a Christian, but asked whether he could still come to church. Graham, of course, said yes. And then, one Sunday evening, Brad sat and listened to a visiting preacher. The message really struck home, and Brad gave his life to Christ.[7]

Back then, there weren't many Christians playing first grade rugby league in Sydney. A lot of people were surprised by Brad's decision—some were impressed, others less so—but he stuck to his commitment. This new direction started to affect how he played on the field, and what he said and did off it. He worked hard to stop swearing, and found that he was developing compassion and patience towards people at the club.

Around this time, a young man named Jason Stevens started playing in the St George first grade side. He, too, would go on to play for New South Wales and Australia. Jason had some knowledge of Christianity but for him, according to Graham, Jesus was "about number 6 in his life". Jason saw that Brad had

---

[7] I should mention that Brad ended up marrying Joanne—and Graham took the wedding.

become a Christian, was very interested in what he saw, and spoke often with him about it.

Jason also got to know Graham, and about a year later found himself in the chaplain's lounge room being taken through the gospel tract *Two Ways to Live*. He, too, gave his life to Christ.

Graham and Joanne (and others) helped Brad come to faith. Graham and Brad (and others) then helped Jason come to faith. At the time of writing, Graham is still an Anglican minister in Sydney. Brad is a fireman and attends church with his family in Sydney's southern suburbs. Jason is also a keen Christian who often appears in the media, has written a book, and recently produced a movie.

With God's help, sport can be a great mission field!

SPORT AND SUPPORT

Sport and spiritual encouragement

> Therefore, as we have opportunity, let us do good to all people, especially to those who belong to the family of believers.
> (Galatians 6:10)

Sally Kopiec is a fencer who coached the Australian wheelchair fencing team around the turn of the century. In this capacity, she was involved with national teams who competed at the Paralympic Games and the World Championships. Now in her 80s, she is still very involved with fencing, coaching, and her local church. A lover of her sport, she has also been keen to live as a Christian in that context—to encourage believers and witness to others where possible.

On one occasion, Sally was attending a competition with the Australian wheelchair fencers in Italy. On a day off, Sally and some members of the Australian and United States teams decided to do some sight-seeing, and so caught the train to Florence. One of the American athletes was Harrison Samuels, an impressive athlete who has represented his country numerous times in wheelchair fencing.

Some way into the journey, and though nothing specific had been said, Harrison turned to Sally and asked whether she was a Christian. She said that she was. Harrison was thrilled. Sally recalls him telling her: "My mother prayed that I'd meet another Christian on this trip. It looks as if her prayers have been answered!" The two of them fell into animated conversation, had a great time of mutual encouragement, and prayed together.

In the years that followed, Sally, Harrison, and some other Christian wheelchair fencers would gather at international competitions for fellowship. They regularly held small services with singing, Bible reading, prayer, and a talk on the Christian life. "We would put up a notice at the competition venue inviting anyone who was interested to attend", says Sally. "It was usually a core group of four—Harrison, a girl named Anja from Germany, a Polish woman Zofia, and me. Over time, however, more came along—both Christians and non-Christians—just to find out what it was all about."[1]

On one occasion, the usually vivacious Anja looked downcast. "She'd lost her bubble," said Sally, "so I asked her what was wrong". Anja explained that, back in Germany, a Christian pastor had encouraged her to attend a healing service and promised that if she went, she would walk again. Anja went to the service, but did not end up walking. The pastor's assessment was that she had not prayed hard enough. Anja was shattered.

---

1 Some of the details relating to these athletes have been changed.

Sally was able to share with her the Bible's teaching on healing—that God sometimes heals miraculously or through 'normal medical treatment', while sometimes he does not. Sally reminded Anja that, regardless of whether or not we are healed, God loves us, Jesus died for us, God has a great plan for each of us, and there will be no wheelchairs in heaven. Anja was greatly encouraged and reaffirmed in her faith.

Friendship and faith

As we said in the previous chapter, one of the best reasons for playing sport is to meet people and make friends. It also provides excellent opportunities to share our faith with those who are not yet followers of Jesus. But sport provides yet another great spiritual opportunity—one that generally gets far less attention than evangelism: sport can be a wonderful platform for building up other believers. The purpose of this chapter is to help us appreciate and take hold of these opportunities.

Paul writes to the Galatians, "Therefore, as we have opportunity, let us do good to all people, especially to those who belong to the family of believers" (Gal 6:10). There are many ways we can 'do good' to other Christian sportspeople. We can provide (and benefit from) friendship, enjoyment, personal support, modelling, mentoring, and organized Christian fellowship. The end result is that we, and others, can be strengthened and spurred on as believers. While this may happen naturally to some extent, it is more likely to be effective if we are deliberate about it.

A sobering truth is that when we spend time with Christians there are two possibilities—we will either end up encouraging them or discouraging them. Let's make it our aim to *en*courage, rather than *dis*courage, the other followers of Jesus whom we meet through sport—to build them up, not tear them down.

Building up believers

The sporting environment lends itself particularly well to the ministry of encouragement, largely because of the amount of time spent together. In many sports, we see our teammates and fellow competitors week after week, and often several times each week. Furthermore, playing sport with others can create a certain bond, with the shared experience resulting in a remarkable connection and closeness. Let's look at some of the specific ways in which we can provide one another with encouragement.

Friendship

We all like to have friends, and if we play a lot of sport it is likely that we will form friendships there. Given that most fellow athletes will not be Christians, it is nice to have a few Christian friends in the mix as well.

One sportsman admitted to me that he felt quite alone as a Christian in his particular situation. Susie Harris described a similar experience during her hockey-playing days. "When I was in the national squad, I spent a lot of my time on my own as a Christian", she says. "I really craved Christian friendships. When I retired from the game in my mid-20s, I went to the

University of Sydney. Almost as soon as I arrived, I joined the Evangelical Union and got really involved. It was so great to finally spend time with other Christians of my own age."

Is there a Christian you know through sport to whom you could be a good friend? And if you are playing sport and in need of a Christian friend, why not pray that God would provide someone? If appropriate, why not take the initiative and ask a Christian friend to join your team or training group?

Enjoyment

Playing sport can be just so enjoyable—particularly playing sport with another believer. Not only can it provide relief from a busy life; it can also provide relief from spiritual conflict. Life is a spiritual battle, and at times the fighting is heavy. Christians can face opposition to their faith at home, at school, at work, at university, from friends, and in their sport. Sometimes it can seem like there is no respite. So what a relief it can be to play sport with another believer or a group of believers—whether it be going for a run together, competing against each other, or playing together in the same team. Playing sport with other believers provides a great opportunity for safe, happy enjoyment.

Support

Not only can Christian sportspeople provide friendship and promote good sports-related enjoyment; they can also be a source of real spiritual support. Simply having another believer around can both comfort us and spur us on. When I was in high school, I was selected in the school's first XI cricket team when I was only 13. I was by far the youngest player in the team. Barely out of primary school, there I was mixing it with older boys who were on the verge of becoming men. To say that I was excited (about being picked) and nervous (about socializing with my seniors) would be an understatement.

There was not only the issue of what I would talk to them about and whether they would be interested in talking to me; there was also the fact that I was a Christian in a predominantly non-Christian team. I say 'predominantly' because there *was* another Christian in the team—Stuart. He was a good cricket and rugby player and attended the same church that I did. Just having him there was a great relief and encouragement. I had the opportunity to watch how an older Christian behaved on and off the field, and he was also friendly towards me. Furthermore, I felt that if I found myself in some sort of problem or ethical dilemma, he would have helped me. I quickly became friendly with the rest of the team, who really were a good bunch of blokes, but it was such a relief to have Stuart there in the early stages.

But we don't just value support when we are young—it's important whatever our age. Our hockey-playing friend Elizabeth Chambers told me: "I found it easier to live out my faith when there was another Christian with me in a team. It meant there was another person there who thought the same as you, who could encourage you and keep you accountable." In particular, she took great strength from meeting with another Christian to read the Bible and pray when they were on the road together.

Sometimes, when there is no other Christian around, there

may be a chaplain. As I write this, Dan Sams is a member of the New South Wales cricket squad. He loves playing the game and values his teammates, but admits that he faces numerous challenges as a believer in a 'boys' club' environment where some players live very luxurious lifestyles. "There are choices I face, temptations I experience, and sacrifices I make that many others do not really understand." However, he says he is very grateful that the state squad has a chaplain. "Simon [the chaplain] has been an unbelievable support to me over the past year. He's been supporting me and helping me to think through issues from the Bible. I need to put God first, then marriage, then relationships. Sport, as much as I love it, must not be number one."

As the writer of Ecclesiastes says:

> Two are better than one,
>   because they have a good return for their labour:
> If either of them falls down,
>   one can help the other up. (Eccl 4:9-10a)

Modelling

Darren Smith played in the Australian National Basketball League from 1994-2004. Speaking in 2000, Darren admitted: "I was a Christian and a basketballer and I felt that they were two different spheres." That was until 1997, when he was asked to join an Athletes in Action team, a squad consisting of Christians mostly from the United States. The team held daily devotions and spent a lot of time praying for each other. These patterns of behaviour had a big impact on Darren. "It was the first time I'd ever done that with basketball players", he said. "That's when I started recognizing that God is in everything—not just outside of basketball, but including basketball."

People are great imitators. Children learn from observing their parents. Teenagers study their peers and their heroes for cues on how to act. In all walks of life and at all ages, we learn by watching and copying others. This is true in the Christian life as well. Paul writes to the Corinthians: "Follow my example, as I follow the example of Christ" (1 Cor 11:1). Paul sought to follow Christ's example and he, in turn, urged the Corinthian Christians to follow his.

Whenever you're involved in sport, look for good examples of Christian sportspeople to model yourself on. Susie Harris, for example, describes how Eric Liddell inspired her when she was growing up. And do your best to be a good example of a Christian playing your sport. Who knows—perhaps someone will model themselves on you!

Mentoring

We can also be quite deliberate about assisting another person in their Christian faith. A more mature Christian will often take it upon themselves to mentor or disciple a newer, younger or less mature believer while they are together in the sporting sphere. This mentoring might be in relation to specific sports-related issues, or it may relate to the Christian life more generally.

David Tyndall is a former Sydney first grade rugby union player and a founding member of Sports and Leisure Ministries in Australia. Over the years, he has been involved in sports ministry on a full-time and part-time basis. David has often found himself in a position where he has been able to mentor younger Christian sportspeople. "They often want assistance on how to be a Christian in a sporting context", he says. "Sportspeople ask questions about such things as how you reconcile being aggressive on the sports field with being a Christian, or whether a Christian should 'walk' in cricket, or should a Christian basketballer deliberately foul when the coach tells them to, or should a Christian scrum-half deliberately feed the ball into the second row. Sometimes the questions can relate more to sporting culture, like: 'What should I do at the club after the game when everyone else is getting stuck into the grog?' It is a great privilege to assist others in talking through very practical issues that Christians face in the sporting arena."

Rugby league international Brad Mackay recalls a situation in which he benefited from the mentoring of an older, more mature Christian—in his case, a former rugby league playing Christian. "Back when I became a believer," Brad recalls, "there were very few Christians in the competition. Today there are a lot more, but back then it was different." As a young believer, Brad was thrilled to meet Ian Barkley, who had been a high-profile player in the 1980s. "Ian was a real help to me", Brad says. "He'd been there and done that. He knew what it was like being a Christian and playing top level league. I could talk to him about issues without having to go into lengthy explanations."

Along with addressing sports-specific issues, mentoring can take place on a more all-encompassing basis. We read in the previous chapter of how God used Lynda Hewitt to help bring fellow hockey player Jill Ireland to the Lord. Lynda did not stop there. After Jill's conversion, Lynda continued to meet with and read the Bible with Jill to help her grow in her new walk with Jesus. She took Jill along to Loughborough University's Christian Union, invited her to lead on a Christian camp, and accompanied her on a Christian mission trip. Later, once Lynda had married, Jill lived with Lynda and her husband for a year as she completed her studies.

As we know, Jill went on to share the gospel with another hockey player who also became a believer—Wendy. "Very simply, I did for Wendy what Lynda had done for me", Jill says. "I prayed for her, we opened the Bible together every week, I shared my life with her, I got to know her, and we loved having fun and hanging out together." Lynda mentored Jill, who mentored Wendy. Paul writes to Timothy of a similar mentoring or training process: "And the things you have heard me say in the presence of many witnesses entrust to reliable people who will also be qualified to teach others" (2 Tim 2:2).

Christian gatherings

One of the great things that Christians can do within their sports is meet regularly for fellowship. These gatherings can help followers of Jesus to stand firm and to reach out with their faith in their particular sporting contexts.

Many large-scale sporting events have Christian Bible studies or church meetings for athletes. During the 2018 Commonwealth Games on the Gold Coast, church meetings were held every morning and evening. Australian long-distance runner Eloise Wellings attended many of these gatherings. "On the Sunday," she said, "there was a big service and there were a couple of hundred people there. It was actually what I'd imagine heaven to look like—people from all different backgrounds and cultures coming together to worship Jesus."

Some sports also have well-organized Christian groups associated with them—for example, Christian Surfers Australia. Other gatherings are more ad hoc. When I first started playing first grade cricket, a small group of past and present Christian cricketers, including Brian Booth, would meet on a semi-regular basis for mutual support and ministry. As a younger cricket-playing believer, I found this very encouraging.

Later, when I was in my mid-20s, one of Brian's sons-in-law—with the support of a few other cricketers, including me—started a small group called Christians in Cricket. We encouraged each other to stand firm in our faith and reach out with our faith in our cricketing circles. We met regularly during the season and occasionally in the off-season.

In cricket, as with all areas of life, there were unique pressures that sought to sideline our Christian faith. But as the writer to the Hebrews says, Christians are to "encourage one another daily, as long as it is called 'Today,' so that none of you may be hardened by sin's deceitfulness" (Heb 3:13). The local church I attended, along with Christians in Cricket, certainly encouraged me and helped me to resist becoming 'hardened'.

Tearing down believers

As with all areas of Christian living, there are dangers as well as opportunities when it comes to playing sport with other believers. It strikes me that there are two main mistakes to avoid—setting a bad example, and wasting opportunities.

Bad examples

Whether we like it or not, we are always serving as an example of how a Christian behaves. The question is: What sort of example are we—a good or a bad one? I don't want to give specific instances of Christians behaving badly, so I have invented a few generic examples which are typical of the sorts of things that can happen.

You are a young sportsperson playing in a team with older people. You know that one of your teammates is a Christian. Because you are new to the team, they don't yet know that you are also a believer. While sitting in the locker room with your team after your first game, wondering how this older Christian will stand out as different, you observe him telling a few dirty jokes, bad-mouthing a player who is not there, and getting increasingly drunk.

You are watching a game in which a Christian is playing. She is consistently and aggressively arguing with the referee and fouling other players. You overhear two non-Christian spectators who have been observing her behaviour: "Apparently, Julie leads singing at her church", one of them says. Both laugh at the apparent absurdity of Julie being part of a church, given her on-field behaviour.

You follow a particular sport in which a high-profile competitor is known to be a Christian. This player often speaks about his faith in churches and schools. That is all very encouraging, up until the time when you read in the press that he has been picked up and charged with drunken and disorderly behaviour outside a nightclub. Later, charges of sexual assault are laid against him. His Christian faith is quickly ridiculed in the media.

How should we think about such behaviour? First, we should recognize it as bad behaviour. It doesn't bring glory to God. It harms others. It harms the player themselves. It is a bad witness to the world, discouraging other believers and setting a bad example for them. A younger or newer Christian may now think it's okay to tell dirty jokes, to bad-mouth others, to behave aggressively, to foul opponents, to disrespect referees, or to get drunk. (Surely no Christian would ever think it was okay to engage in sexual assault!) And if a younger Christian did not actually think it's acceptable to do these things, they may conclude, "So it's wrong, but everyone does it", and find it harder to resist the temptation to engage in such practices themselves.

Jesus highlights the serious impact that our words and actions can have upon others: "If anyone causes one of these little ones—those who believe in me—to stumble, it would be better for them if a large millstone were hung around their neck and they were thrown into the sea" (Mark 9:42). Now, of course, Christians *are* forgiven for their sins—including for the kinds of bad behaviour in my examples—but God is still seriously displeased with such actions, and they do have significant consequences.

While we will recognise such behaviour as being bad and

contrary to God's will for how his people should live, we shouldn't be overly surprised by it. As Jeremiah 17:9 says, "The heart is deceitful above all things and beyond cure. Who can understand it?" Now, of course, Christian believers are forgiven for their sins and the Holy Spirit is working to progressively cure our heart and make us more like Christ. But, this side of heaven, we will still struggle with and succumb to sin, both in private and public ways.

Furthermore, we don't want to become self-righteous. We should be very much aware of our own sinful shortcomings: "all have sinned and fall short of the glory of God" (Rom 3:23). We should be thankful for the grace of God shown in the death of his Son, which provides the forgiveness of sins for all who believe—for our sins, for the sins of other offending sportspeople, and for anyone else who turns to him in faith. As we have said a few times now, thank God that we are saved by his grace, not by our works (Eph 2:8-9).

Finally, the Christian life isn't simply about each person merely looking out for their own interests. As Paul tells us in Galatians 6, we must always be looking to help one another: "Carry each other's burdens, and in this way you will fulfil the law of Christ" (Gal 6:2). So each of us must be keen to do whatever we can to help other believers who are struggling spiritually. This can involve providing personal assistance (if we know the person) and praying for them (whether we know them personally or not).

While we can often learn a lot from other Christian sportspeople, we need to remember that they are not perfect and that, ultimately, Jesus is our role model for life.

Wasting opportunities

Another danger is to simply waste the opportunities for Christian encouragement that sport provides. We go to sport, we play sport, we come home, and the spiritual opportunities never really register with us. We don't take up opportunities to encourage, support and have fellowship with other Christian sportspeople. The mere fact that we may play in a Christian football team does not mean that we are spiritually encouraging the other believers in our team. The mere fact that there may be another Christian at your netball club does not mean that you are helping her to grow in her faith. We need to actively think and pray about how we can "spur one another on toward love and good deeds" (Heb 10:24). Are there other Christians in your sporting circles whom you could seek to encourage?

Conclusion

Some athletes participate in sports where travelling for extended periods to train and compete can make regular church attendance difficult. To provide supplementary Bible teaching, fellowship and support, church gatherings and Bible studies are often held alongside major sporting events. Jules Wilkinson, part-time staff worker with Christians in Sport, assists with this ministry on the European track and field circuit, having a particular focus on the female athletes.

Jules recalls one evening before a major women's final at a Diamond League meet a few years back. A Bible study for athletes was scheduled, and several of the women running in the next day's final would normally have attended. Jules was aware that finishing positions in the final would have significant financial implications for the women, so she wondered: will they turn up the night before such an important race?

In the end, about six of the finalists came along. While some might assume there would have been an element of wariness between the women given what was at stake the following day, what happened was quite the opposite. "As we met together that night," recalls Jules, "there was a real feeling of friendship and mutual support as we looked at God's word and had fellowship. They might be rival competitors on the track, but they were first and foremost sisters in Christ."

With God's help, sport can be a great place for encouragement and spiritual support. Who can you assist?

BUT THERE'S MORE...

The potential benefits of good health and travel

For physical training is of some value, but godliness has value for all things, holding promise for both the present life and the life to come. (1 Timothy 4:8)

Good health

The life of a professional footballer places a high premium on physical fitness. Training sessions can be gruelling, games are long and intense, and aspects of life such as diet and sleep patterns require constant, careful attention. Being fit is important for the team, for the player's individual performance and, as a result, for their personal livelihood. But fitness also has significant personal benefits as well. Linvoy Primus, the former Portsmouth defender whom we first met back in chapter 3, reflects back on his playing days: "You can take it for granted at the time, but being fit gave me a clarity of thought and a sense of feeling strong and athletic. It was a good feeling."

Now retired from the game, Linvoy still tries to keep in good physical shape. It's not part of his job anymore, so he has to fit exercise into his weekly routine. What motivates him to stay healthy? "If I exercise, I feel mentally and physically fresher. If I don't, I feel tired. Maintaining a level of fitness not only feels great but also allows me to fit into the same clothes!"

Establishing and maintaining good health can be one of the real positives of sport. It's one of the reasons that parents encourage their children to take part. What mum or dad doesn't like to see their kids running around outside and then coming inside exhausted but happy? Health is also one of the reasons that many adults play sport. Jogging, swimming, cycling and going to the gym are popular, while those who find those pursuits a little non-motivating can happily run themselves to exhaustion chasing a ball around a field or court.

The Latin phrase *nens sana in corpore sano* expresses the ideal for many. It is usually translated as 'a healthy mind in a healthy body', and can be understood to express the view that a healthy body can *promote* a healthy mind.

The Mental Health Foundation (UK) would agree. It tells us that physical and mental health should not be thought of as two separate things. "Poor physical health can lead to an increased risk of developing mental health problems. Similarly, poor mental health can negatively impact on physical health, leading to an increased risk of some conditions."[1] I

---

[1] 'Physical health and mental health', *Mental Health Foundation*: mentalhealth.org.uk/a-to-z/p/physical-health-and-mental-health.

can certainly testify to feeling better and working better when I am at least moderately fit.

A healthy mind in a healthy body

Sport can improve our level of physical fitness and, in turn, our general wellbeing. When we are healthy, we usually have more energy, feel better, look better, think more effectively, possess better mental health, and live longer. For the Christian, this will help us in our efforts to love God and to love others. A basic level of good health should assist concentration during times of Bible study and prayer. It can also help our ministry—we are more likely to put our best foot forward when helping to run Friday night youth group at the end of a tiring week if we possess a basic level of fitness. And being less tired and run down should help us to display Christian character in our relationships. How many of us do and say things we regret when we are feeling second rate?

Of course, the Holy Spirit is the person who really makes a difference in our lives, but God also works through normal physiological processes. We don't know what specific things Paul had in mind when he wrote that "physical training is of some value" (1 Tim 4:8), but it is likely that the benefits of good health were among them.

Why not make a point of maintaining a reasonable level of physical fitness? It might be through some sort of exercise program, participation in a sport, or (as for me) through a combination of both. For those of us who are busy (and, let's face it, who isn't?), the thing to do is to work it into our weekly schedule.

An unhealthy body—and mind

Sadly, there is the other side of the coin. Sport, like all good things in life, has been impacted by the Fall, which means it does *not* always promote good health. Injuries will regularly come our way, certain sports can pose serious long-term health risks, and at higher levels of competition there may even be the temptation to use performance-enhancing drugs. Let's briefly consider each of these challenges.

Dealing with injuries

Injuries are a perennial problem for the sportsperson. Even the most casual participant of a few years standing should be able to reel off a litany of stresses, strains and snaps. These can be painful (both the injury and the treatment) and disappointing (as we miss games, races and exercise). For some, injuries can be truly devastating—a long-hoped-for dream can vanish in a moment or a sporting career can go up in smoke.

Alan Comfort was converted at the age of 20 when playing football with Cambridge United. He subsequently transferred to Leyton Orient and then Middlesbrough. In 1989, aged 25, Alan had grown in his Christian faith, he was playing well on the field, his wife was pregnant with their first child, and they had just moved into a lovely house. Things were looking good. Then, on the third of November, Middlesbrough was playing away at Newcastle. Alan's team was up 2-1 in the second half when he went in for a regulation tackle. His studs caught in the ground, his knee twisted, he heard a snap, and he was stretchered from the field. It was a career-ending cruciate ligament injury. It happened as quickly as that—no warning, no opportunity to prepare. "I did trust God," Alan has written, "but this was not a pleasant period of my life".[2]

Another elite athlete to experience the trials of injury is Eloise Wellings, an Australian long-distance runner. In 2000, as a 16-year-old and still in her second-last year of high school, she qualified for the Olympic Games in Sydney. Yet not long before the start of the Games, she developed a stress fracture in her hip and never had the chance to compete. Eloise also missed the 2004 and 2008 Olympics through injury. Thankfully, she competed in the 2012 and 2016 Games.

Eloise's career has been dogged by stress fractures—eleven, to be precise. Yet God can work good through adversity. While never enjoying them at the time, Eloise now reflects on all she has learned through her injuries. "I became a Christian through my first stress fracture", she says. "When I qualified for the Sydney Olympics and three weeks later developed my first stress fracture, I was devastated. At school, I withdrew into myself and isolated myself from my friends. Then one day a new girl came up to me and said, 'Eloise, I've been praying for you, and so have some of my friends from church. God has a great plan for your life!'

"I had always believed in God, but had a warped idea of who he was at the time. I thought that the injury meant that I was being punished for something. I had no real appreciation of God's love and grace, of how he wanted a relationship

---

2   Alan Comfort, 'Shall We Sing a Song for You', in Jeffrey Heskins and Matt Baker (eds), *Footballing Lives: As Seen by Chaplains in the Beautiful Game*, Canterbury Press Norwich, London, 2006, pp. 29-31 (quote from p. 31).

with me, or of how he cared about the intricate details of my life." Eloise started to go along to church, and before long "the lights went on" and she became a follower of Jesus.

She now understands that God has used the injuries over the years to strengthen her faith. "I've seen what God has done through them", she says. "Each time I cling to Romans 8:28: 'And we know that in all things God works for the good of those who love him, who have been called according to his purpose'. While I didn't enjoy them at the time, I wouldn't take any injury away. I have learned so much from them."

Any athlete needs to accept that injuries *will* happen. We can do our best to prevent them, to minimize their impact and to recover from them, but they will happen. When they do, we should look to God, trust in him, and trust that he will use the situation for good—even if we can't see it at the time.

Long-term dangers
Sport can—and usually does—promote our physical and mental wellbeing, but it is too simplistic to say that sports *only* promote good health, or that *all* sports promote good health. Many have potential physical side effects over and above the general threat of strained muscles, ligaments and tendons. These may include the long-term effects of a high-speed clash of bodies, taking a serious fall, or being struck by a ball or other piece of sporting equipment. Some sports are more prone to these sorts of injuries than others. Take, for example, everything we now know about the tragic, long-term effect of head injuries among NFL players. Not only have an increasing number of retired players developed dementia and Alzheimer's Disease;

many have also experienced a horrible condition known as CTE—a progressive degenerative disease of the brain, whose symptoms include depression, aggression and disorientation.[3]

Wisdom demands that our decision on whether to take part in a particular sport should therefore include an assessment of its potential to benefit or harm our long-term mental and physical wellbeing.

Performance-enhancing drugs
Of course, so-called recreational drugs are a temptation for many people, whether they play sport or not. For people in certain sports, however, there is the additional temptation to use performance-enhancing drugs (PEDs). The lure is greatest for those competing at the highest levels, where the desire to succeed can often become almost consuming. In some sports, PED use appears to verge on the endemic. But taking illegal substances is not only cheating; it also has very negative long-term effects on one's health.

In chapter 5, we looked at the results of the survey conducted by American physician Bob Goldman, who asked 198 athletes if they would take a banned drug if they were guaranteed to win every event for the next five years without being caught, then die from the side effects. Remember, over half said that they would. Clearly, the temptation to use PEDs is very powerful.

I remember competing in the under-20 shot put at the

---

3   CTE stands for chronic traumatic encephalopathy. See 'NFL Concussions Fast Facts', *CNN.com*, 15 August 2019: edition.cnn.com/2013/08/30/us/nfl-concussions-fast-facts/index.html.

Australian Track and Field Championships against Werner Reiterer, an extremely talented thrower from Victoria. While he won the event, discus was his specialty. He went on to compete in the discus at two Olympic Games, won a Commonwealth Games gold medal, and was eight times national champion in this event. But Werner quit the sport just before the Sydney Olympics and wrote a book called *Positive*, in which he admitted to five years' abuse of PEDs.[4] He asserted that this was "a last-ditch response to a sports world so awash with drugs that natural athletes—who are in the minority, just a few percent, he said, in some events—either succumb or compete without real hope of success".[5]

Many might think that a Christian would never deliberately take banned substances, but this is to downplay the force of the temptation and the deceitfulness of the human heart. Let me be clear: it is *never* right for anyone—Christian or otherwise—to take an illegal PED. If you feel the pressure to do so—whether it be at your coach's suggestion, or simply from your own desire to succeed—I would urge you to pray, and to seek the support of a wise Christian. If you do not think you will be able to resist taking the banned substance if you remain in your particular sporting context, you will need to remove yourself from it.

---

4   Werner Reiterer, *Positive: An Australian Olympian Reveals the Inside Story of Drugs and Sport*, Macmillan, Sydney, 2000.
5   Daniel Williams, 'Bad News Bearer', *TIME*, 5 March 2001: content.time.com/time/world/article/0,8599,2056102,00.html.

Travel

Play sport and see the world! Or at least see more of the world than you would otherwise have seen.

Growing up, sport took me all over Sydney. I became increasingly familiar with parts of the city that I would not otherwise have known, and met people I would not otherwise have met. Eventually I found myself in cricket, football and athletics squads that travelled further afield, touring into regional New South Wales and even going interstate. I really enjoyed these experiences—spending extended time with teammates and seeing new places. When I was 20, sport took me to London for five months as I played a season of cricket in the Middlesex League. This proved to be one of the seminal experiences of my life. While in London, I joined a great church, played plenty of sport, met lots of great people, and took the opportunity to explore Great Britain and parts of Europe.

I love travel, and I am very thankful to God for the opportunities he has given me.[6] My travel experiences have taught me that wherever we go—within our country or overseas—God is there with us. I think of Psalm 139:9-10 as my travel verses:

> **If I rise on the wings of the dawn,**
> **if I settle on the far side of the sea,**
> **even there your hand will guide me,**
> **your right hand will hold me fast.**

---

6 I have written elsewhere in much more detail about the potential benefits and dangers of travel in my book *Travelling the World as Citizens of Heaven* (Matthias Media, Sydney, 2017). As with sport, travel, if undertaken in a godly way with the gospel at the centre of our plans, can be a real plus for one's spiritual life and for the kingdom of God.

These verses are a great encouragement to me. However, for all the potential benefits of travelling and touring with sport, it also has its dangers, and we need to be alert to these. Let's think about the benefits first.

The benefits of travel

It has been said, "The world is a book, and those who do not travel read only a page". There is nothing wrong with reading only a page—we don't *need* to travel! But if sport *does* give us the chance to 'read a bit more', it can be a real privilege.

"I saw a lot of the world in a few years", says former Australian hockey international Susie Harris. "I made the Australian squad at 17 years of age, and over the next five years hockey took me to the four corners of the globe. I visited England, Scotland, Ireland, Holland, Germany, Spain, the United States, Canada, Argentina, Chile, Asia and New Zealand. I loved it! I would get a little homesick, but I always wanted to go. I recall a day off in Chile when we were driving through the Andes in a rickety bus. There was a steep precipice on one side of the road as we traversed the rugged alpine cliffs. Looking around at the view, it felt like we were floating in snow. Travel was full of moments like this."

Touring with a team also provides a great opportunity to spend extended time with people, particularly teammates. In normal life, we may see our teammates at the game each week and perhaps at training on one or two evenings in between. When on tour, we are together 24/7. Relationships can deepen very quickly, and there are many opportunities for memorable shared experiences. We've already discussed the many ways in which sport also provides opportunities for evangelism and spiritual support, and travelling together can significantly accelerate and enhance these opportunities.

Former Oxford University rugby player and now Church of England minister Pete Nicholas found himself on a rugby tour of Japan not long after his conversion. Another member of the squad was a Christian and, while away, they were able to encourage and spur each other on in their faith. During the trip, word quickly spread among the tour group that Pete had found God. This sparked endless conversations about his new beliefs, with reactions ranging from discomfort to real interest. Some were seeking to the extent that Pete ended up reading the Bible with them. The following Christmas, about half the team attended a Christmas Carols service with him.

I have also found that travelling with sport has given me the chance to grow in my relationship with God, stand out as different in my behaviour, and to speak about my faith. My five months in England playing cricket were a great opportunity. Away from the familiarity of home, I relied more obviously on God. I prayed that God would lead me to Christians to encourage, and to interested non-Christians to whom I could speak about my faith. Both of these things happened.

The cricket club I played for in England was full of interesting people and great characters, but I was not aware of any who would have considered themselves to be born again believers. Like many similar sporting organizations, it was very much a 'boys' club'—most players drank more than I did, and their attitudes to many things, including women, were often very different from mine.

Romans 13:13 says, "Let us behave decently, as in the daytime, not in carousing and drunkenness, not in sexual immorality and debauchery, not in dissension and jealousy". These are words to bear in mind when touring or travelling with sport. As I said earlier, when I was about 18 I resolved not to have more than two alcoholic drinks on any one occasion, and I applied this during my time in England (as I have since). I also endeavoured to be friendly and honourable in the way I related to the women I met. The difference in my behaviour, and my references to my Christian faith, sometimes provoked spiritual discussions with teammates.

But travelling with sport is not always a holiday adventure. If frequently undertaken, the novelty can wear off and it becomes routine—perhaps even a grind. We miss the comforts, conveniences and friendships of home. We can miss the consistent Bible teaching and fellowship of our normal church. And, if a sportsperson is married with children (or perhaps in a serious relationship), being away for extended periods can be heart-wrenching.

If you are doing what you believe God wants you to do and you find yourself travelling with sport—whether it be occasionally or regularly—embrace the opportunities, seek God's support through the hardships, and (as we are about to discuss) beware of the dangers. God has you there for a reason—make the most of it.

The dangers of travel

For all its opportunities and benefits, travelling or touring with sport can expose us to many dangers. Being away from our home, our church and our normal support structures can ask some questions of our relationship with God. Will we still read the Bible and pray while we are away? This is absolutely vital. If we are away for more than a few days, will we seek out Christian fellowship? This is clearly desirable even if we are only travelling for a short period of time, and essential if we're away from home for a longer stretch of time (Heb 10:24-25). Being away from home can drive us to become more obviously dependent on God. It can also drive us away from him. If you are travelling as part of your sport, resolve firmly before leaving to spend time with God each day in Bible reflection and prayer!

Former Australian volleyball captain Priscilla Ruddle, now a missionary in West Africa, recalls the amount of time she spent travelling with her sport. "When I spent longer periods of time overseas without access to a local church, it would have been easy to drift. But God was gracious and helped me to see the importance of spending time in his word, whether that be listening to sermons (in those days on tapes or MP3s), personal Bible study, or reading helpful books. True to his word and through the work of the Holy Spirit, God continued to guide and hold me."

Pete Nicholas says he is aware of many Christians who have participated in things on sporting tours that they have subsequently come to regret and over which they have felt great shame. Of course, as Christians we all make mistakes and God forgives us for our sins, but it is much better if we can avoid the blunders in the first place.

The following is a summary of some advice Pete has for Christians going on sports tours:

- » Make it known right from the start that you are a Christian. This will shape other people's expectations of what you might do or not do.
- » Set boundaries for your behaviour (for example, your policy on drinking alcohol) early on. Know your limits, be proactive about the problems you may encounter, and make sure you resolve to avoid doing things that might make you particularly susceptible to sin.
- » Organize support and accountability. If there is another Christian on tour, resolve to pray together, read the Bible together, and generally look out for each other. If there is no other believer, organize some support from back home via email, Skype, or the like.

Travelling with sport has its plusses and minuses. Resolve to embrace the opportunities and avoid the dangers.

THE SPORT CYCLE

Starting out, getting serious, finishing up... and beyond

"The city streets will be filled with boys and girls playing there." (Zechariah 8:5)

///

Growing up, life was all about sport for Nick Farr-Jones. The second child in a family of three boys, he was perpetually in the backyard of his southern Sydney home playing any one of a number of games. His interest in such physical pursuits was further fanned into flame when he was sent to Newington College for high school. The school was blessed with good facilities and coaches, and Nick revelled in the rich sporting environment, excelling in athletics and rugby (although, now quite famously, he did not make the rugby first XV).[1]

At age 16, while he was a student at Newington, Nick went along to a local church. Originally motivated by his interest in

---

1 Some of the information in this section comes from Peter Fitz-simons, *Nick Farr-Jones: The Authorised Biography*, Random House, Sydney, 1993.

a couple of girls who attended, he heard the gospel preached and saw how it changed people's lives. He became convinced of the truth of the message, recognized its appeal, and became a follower of Jesus.

School led on to tertiary studies at the University of Sydney, where he studied law. It was here that his rugby really took off. In his second year, he was promoted to the university's first grade team. Over the next few years, Nick began to realize that he might get somewhere in rugby, and resolved to go for it. He loved the game, the on-field camaraderie, and the off-field socializing.

At the age of 22, he was selected to tour Europe with the Australian team, and in late 1984 made his international debut against England at Twickenham. It was the start of a career that would see him play on 63 occasions for his country, 36 times as captain. In 1991, he led the team to victory in the World Cup.

Soon after, Nick realized that his time in top level rugby was drawing to a close. "I was married with a child, rugby was not my livelihood [Nick worked as a lawyer, rugby still being an amateur sport at the time], and I felt that the time had come." Having just experienced the thrill of a World Cup victory, the plan was to retire after the tour of South Africa in 1992. "It was two years after Nelson Mandela had been released from prison and the African National Congress supported the tour", says Nick. "I had not played there before, and I thought it would be a good way to finish up." He reflects, "While I was comfortable with the decision to retire, it was still a very emotional thing to do."

Nick's life did not stop there. These days, he is a family man with four children, is involved with his church, works for a funds management company, and does some television commentary. He is often asked to speak at Christian events where he enjoys encouraging people in their lives, particularly in their Christian faith. He has also had the opportunity to devote time to a number of worthy causes and not-for-profit organizations. He has served on various boards, was a Chairman of the New South Wales Rugby Union, and is Chairman of Stand Tall—an organization co-founded by his wife, Angie—which aims to motivate young Australians to make positive life choices, and raises funds for Wesley Mission's work with the homeless.

Amidst his many commitments, Nick's devotional life is very important to him. He aims to have his quiet times early in the morning. When I spoke with him, he told me, "I've been focusing on Jesus in the garden of Gethsemane. What he suffered for us was incredible! He asked for the cup to be taken from him if possible, but throughout it all remained obedient to the will of his Father."

As with participation in sport at all levels, Nick's rugby career followed the standard sporting cycle—starting out, playing the game (and, in his case, getting serious about it), and finishing up. This chapter addresses a few of the issues relating to each stage of this cycle, as well as what happens next.

Starting out

Like Nick, most of us start out with sport when we're young. The motivation may come from parents, siblings, friends, school or television, and before long it becomes part of our life. Of course, many take up sport (especially particular sports, like jogging, golf and lawn bowls) later in life. I only started trying to teach myself to throw the hammer in very recent years. But the sporting cycle most commonly begins in our school days.

Upon trying a sport, if we *like* it—if it is fun, if we enjoy competition, if we enjoy pushing ourselves, if we enjoy being part of a team, if we experience some success, and perhaps (if we are spiritually minded) if we feel that it fits well into our Christian life—we will usually continue playing, circumstances permitting. At this point, take on board and apply the things discussed in this book so far—work on your relationship with God, be aware of the opportunities and dangers, seek to glorify God in your words and actions, and enjoy the journey.

For most sports-loving people, sport remains a leisure time pursuit. But for some—for the particularly talented—an additional issue can arise: a period of time is reached during which they face the decision of whether they will attempt to take their sport more seriously with a view to perhaps turning professional and making a career out of it. While there are many sports-related careers such as coach, umpire, and administrator, we will focus here on some of the issues facing a person who is considering pursuing a career *competing* as a professional athlete.

Getting serious

Having the option of pursuing sport as a possible career can be a very exciting situation in which to find one's self. What young sportsperson doesn't dream of playing for their country or their favourite club and getting paid to do so? Furthermore, having a Christian presence in top-level sport can be wonderful for the kingdom of God. David Sheppard, the former English test cricketer and later Bishop of Liverpool, once wrote: "I believe that He [i.e. God] wants His followers in the middle of every walk of life, and I am persuaded that it was His will for me to give some years to playing cricket."[2]

The stage of life at which an athlete must make the decision of whether to pursue their dream can vary from person to person. Depending on the country and sport, the decision period may come when the sportsperson is still quite young, perhaps not even in their teens. This could be the case, for example, with swimming and gymnastics. In this situation, the decisions are really made by the parents in consultation with the child.[3]

This raises an important issue for the Christian parent: what should they do if their child is talented and has the chance to pursue sport at a serious level? Jules Wilkinson, staff member for Christians in Sport in the UK, faced this very dilemma as a parent. "You get your kids into sport because you like it. It's healthy, it teaches them how to win and lose, it teaches them

---

2 David Sheppard, *Parson's Pitch*, Hodder & Stoughton, London, 1964, p. 52.
3 Christians in Sport in the UK provides support and resources for young athletes who are on a pathway towards elite sport, and for their parents and guardians, with a view to helping them to navigate this tricky process. One excellent resource is available online at christiansinsport.org.uk/resources/how-do-i-support-my-child-as-a-christian-in-the-world-of-elite-sport/.

how to be part of a team, and it keeps them off the streets", she says. "Then, if they prove to be good at it, they start to get selected in teams and attend training camps and the like. Before long, you may realize that your child is on the performance pathway for their sport, and that decisions need to be made that impact upon whether they will be able to pursue the sport seriously. It is rarely straightforward, and the decisions can be both difficult and complicated. If you decide to go for it, then you are on a treadmill. It is a big-time commitment for you and your children, it significantly impacts upon how your family works, and it may even impact on Sunday church attendance."

Clearly, the parents, in consultation with the child, need to make godly, informed decisions shaped by prayerful deliberation. They will need to consider: Do we want to put in the effort that will be required? How will it affect our education, our home life, and our social life? And most importantly: How will it impact our Christian lives, particularly our involvement in regular fellowship? The answers to these questions can be vastly different from one sport to the next. Thankfully, the believer has access to divine wisdom, which will help them to make wise, godly decisions. We gain this wisdom as we engage in genuine Bible-based thought, prayer and discussion.

In other sports, the consideration may not come until a little later—perhaps when the athlete is 18 years of age, or even older. In this situation, the athlete is more able to address the issue for himself or herself, although parents may still play an important advisory role. For most sports, I suspect, the key decisions would occur somewhere in the athlete's mid-teenage years.

In my case, the genuine possibility of pursuing sport professionally dawned on me when I was about 15. Like so many boys, I dreamed of representing my country in cricket. As a youngster, I played the game with great enthusiasm but thought that my dream was probably just that—a dream. I was a handy player, but far from being a prodigy. But then things started to change—and quickly. I was chosen for the under-14 representative team for my area and finished as the team's top wicket-taker. The next year, I was one of the best fast bowlers for my age in the state. When I made the New South Wales under-16 team as opening bowler, a career in cricket was now a definite possibility. By the time I finished school, the serious pursuit of athletics and rugby league also presented themselves as options, but cricket was my first love, so I decided to focus there. I was playing Sydney first grade cricket by the age of 18, and gained selection in the New South Wales under-19 side.

Most importantly, thanks to God, throughout this time I was a Christian and was very involved in my local church. I read my Bible, prayed, sought to encourage other Christians, and tried to be a good witness to those who didn't know Jesus. If you had asked me as an 18-year-old, I would have said that serving God was the most important thing in my life. I would have added that I wanted to become a professional cricketer because I liked it, because I thought it would be a good way to make a living, and because I believed it would be good to have some prominent Christians in the sport. I figured that I could use my position to point people towards Jesus.

Seriously pursuing cricket over the next few years meant that I trained hard, played a lot, and strived to do my best. In my efforts to improve, I organized bowling coaches at various times, and went off to play a season in England. I did all of this with a lot of prayer and with significant support from my parents.

While all this was taking place, I entered university. I worked hard at my studies, but in my mind it was a back-up plan in case cricket did not work, or to provide an option for life after cricket.

Based on my own experience, and having spent time with many Christians who are professional athletes (or aspiring professional athletes) over the years, I would urge the Christian sportsperson (and parents, as appropriate) to take the following steps. (Much of what follows will also apply to those who aren't considering turning professional but who are still dedicating lots of time to their chosen sport and taking it very seriously.)

Step 1: Maintain a close relationship with God

I know I've offered the same advice many times throughout this book already, and it may sound a little like an insight from Captain Obvious, but good coaches come back to the fundamentals time and time again. We are best able to see the world as God sees it, to think well, and to make wise decisions when we are in a close relationship with God. This means doing the sorts of things described in chapter 3—reading God's word, praying, maintaining regular Christian fellowship, and seeking to serve God in whatever ways we can. Making it as an elite athlete requires great discipline; we should apply at least the same degree of discipline to our walk with the Lord.

Step 2: Inform yourself of the opportunities and benefits provided by professional sport

We've already discussed many of the positives associated with sport. The benefits associated with *professional* sport will include many of these, some being experienced at higher levels. For example, if you achieve a degree of fame, your Christian witness and encouragement has the potential to influence a wider range of people.

Professional sport also has the advantage of allowing us to make a living out of doing something we enjoy or find satisfying. That said, when one earns their livelihood from a sport, it may become a little less like *fun* and a lot more like *work*. Still, if it is approached well with biblical priorities to the fore, professional sport can be a great way to live and serve God for a number of years. Former Olympic rower Debbie Flood agrees. "Sure, it was hard at times, but they were great years", she says. "Getting paid to do something I enjoyed and that I found challenging was brilliant. The friendships, the training, the big races, the chance to live out my Christian faith—I loved it."

Step 3: Inform yourself of the dangers and difficulties associated with professional sport

While professional sport offers numerous benefits, it also presents many dangers. This, of course, is true of any job. While we've already discussed many of the sports-related challenges in preceding chapters, some will be experienced by the professional at a heightened level. For example, there is an increased danger of finding one's sense of identity and self-worth in sport rather than in Christ. In addition, professional sport has its distinctive challenges. I will go into a little more detail here than I did with the positive aspects discussed above—not because I think there are more negatives than positives, but because the negatives are often a little less apparent to the young sportsperson.

As with some other careers, professional sport may make regular Sunday fellowship difficult. Playing at the top level often involves Sunday training, Sunday competition, and travelling away from home for extended periods of time. The extent to which this applies varies from sport to sport. While rugby league player Brad Mackay says he was able to get to church most weeks when he was playing, a professional tennis or golf player may be away from home for many months of the year, which means alternative forms of fellowship will be needed—for example, meeting regularly with a sports chaplain or with a Bible-reading/prayer partner. These days, it is quite easy for an athlete to keep in contact with their home church via electronic communication and social media, but this requires some discipline. If regular fellowship of some sort is *just not possible*, it may be best to discontinue playing the sport at that level. While it is highly unlikely to come down to this, the option should always be on the table. As Jesus said, "What good will it be for someone to gain the whole world, yet forfeit their soul?" (Matt 16:26).

Professional sport can also make important relationships difficult. A Christian, of course, should only date another Christian, but spending most of your time in a sporting subculture with no (or few) Christians can make it hard to meet an appropriate person. Furthermore, if you are relatively famous, people (Christians included) may want to date you because of your fame, rather than because of who you are.

If you are married, other challenges present themselves. It can sometimes be difficult to maintain a stable family life if you spend extended periods away from home. Again, electronic communication and social media can be a great help here, but nothing replaces being together in person. Furthermore, some may find having a famous spouse or parent a little daunting as it impinges upon their privacy. That said, having a famous spouse or parent can have its advantages.

Professional sport can also be an insecure sort of existence. Linvoy Primus describes how the vast majority of aspiring footballers never actually sign a professional contract. And for those that do, there is the pressure of getting into the first team, then staying there. Even for those who are playing regular first team football, there is the pressure to sign a better contract and move to a bigger club. There are also the threats of being dropped from the team, being released by a club, or being injured. When your livelihood (and, often, your family's livelihood) depends upon continued performance at a high level, it can be quite a pressured environment.

Finally, there is the danger of being either misunderstood or idolized by some Christians. Some may disapprove of the time dedicated to sport—up until the time when the sportsperson becomes famous, at which point it is suddenly great! Some Christians may be keen to have the sportsperson give their testimony in public, even if the athlete's faith is not yet sufficiently mature to warrant this. You may know of young Christian sportspeople who were put up on a pedestal too early and then fell badly, and very publicly, from grace.

Do these challenges mean that Christians should avoid professional sport? Not at all! Every career has its challenges. But it does mean that the budding professional (and their parents) should be aware of, and prepare for, what may lie ahead.

Step 4: Consult your parents and other wise Christians

Consulting with your parents is always a good thing to do, but especially if you're making big decisions at a young age. They probably know you much better than anyone else and are extremely interested in your welfare. The Bible urges us to honour our parents (Exod 20:12), to listen to their instruction and teaching (Prov 1:8), and to obey them (Eph 6:1). Get your parents' wisdom on your plans.

In addition, Proverbs 12:15 teaches that "the wise listen to advice". Make sure you consult with wise Christians—perhaps the pastor of your church, or a Bible-believing chaplain connected with your sport. Acquaint them with your situation as best you can, and seek their counsel. You particularly want others to help you see how the Scriptures inform your decision.

Step 5: Consult people who know the sport

Again, it is important to listen to wise advice. Even if your coach or some other sporting expert is not a believer, they should still have valuable wisdom and insights to share with you. This may include a realistic assessment of your ability and your chances of getting somewhere in the sport. Depending upon their experience, they may also be able to give you genuine insight into the life of a professional in your chosen field.

Step 6: Prayerfully seek to make wise decisions

This final step speaks for itself. Do your best to be wise—God can ask nothing more of us. To those who are particularly anxious about making poor decisions, Philippians 4:6-7 is helpful:

> Do not be anxious about anything, but in every situation, by prayer and petition, with thanksgiving, present your requests to God. And the peace of God, which transcends all understanding, will guard your hearts and your minds in Christ Jesus.

If, at some stage in the future, you think you may have made an unwise decision for whatever reason—well, we all make mistakes, and God is a gracious and forgiving God! Furthermore, God can even bring good things out of our poor decisions.

What if you don't make it?

Some of the Christians described in this book pursued their sport seriously and made it as professional athletes. Others, such as I, did not. In fact, a majority of those who aspire to reach the highest levels will never make it. If that happens, that does not mean that our efforts have been wasted. God will have used our time in sport to mature us, to make an impact upon others through us, and to give us great experiences along the way. With God, nothing ever goes to waste (Rom 8:28).

Finishing up

One way or another, the sport cycle ends in the same place for every single athlete: finishing up. After all, as the old saying goes, "Father Time is undefeated".

We might retire from playing a sport for a whole variety of reasons. We may simply get tired of our sport, or find that we would rather do something else. We may need to step away due to increased family responsibilities. Perhaps we are dropped from a team or can no longer perform at the level we want, which prompts the decision. Retirement may be forced upon us through injury, or simply through our bodies ageing and gradually wearing out.

Retirement can produce a range of responses. We may experience anything from relief to slight sadness right through to depression. For a person whose self-identity has been caught up in their sport, retirement can prompt the question, "Who am I?" If someone has been part of a team, they may, in some sense, lose their 'family'. They may miss the discipline of training and the thrill of the big match or race. A retired professional sportsperson may miss living in the limelight. They may no longer feel valued. They may wonder what life now holds for them. Or perhaps they may feel as if they have gone from being 'ahead of their peers' in sport to being 'behind their peers' in 'normal life'. Usually, the bigger the role that sport has played in a person's life, the bigger the impact of retirement.

As Christians, we are not immune from some level of retirement-related grief. I stopped playing weekend football a few years back due to frequent injury, and I miss kicking a ball around on a fresh winter's afternoon. Adjusting to retirement from cricket was a little harder, given my greater emotional investment in it.

As mentioned earlier, when Nick Farr-Jones retired from

international rugby he had his faith, his family, and his career in law. Despite that, he says that he still found the move emotional. David Simmons went to theological college after retiring from rugby league and is now very happily working part-time at a church in Sydney and part-time as a rugby league club chaplain. Yet he still admits to feeling the absence of intense competition. "It was thrilling", he says. "When you leave, there is nothing that gives you quite the same buzz."

So, how can a Christian sportsperson 'retire well'? Let me offer five specific suggestions.

Suggestion 1: Maintain a close relationship with God

As has been emphasized throughout this book, we do best in all areas of life when we are in a close relationship with God. This will help us approach and deal with retirement from a sport in a number of ways. For example, it will help us to better appreciate that our identity and self-worth is in Christ. It's especially important to spend significant time in prayer. Give thanks to God for your life in sport, and pray that he will help you to transition well into life after sport.

Suggestion 2: Get the support of other Christians you trust

This is particularly helpful if you anticipate that retiring from your sport may be a difficult process for you.

Suggestion 3: Plan and prepare for what you will do next

Give some advance thought to what you will do next. If the sport is more at the level of hobby, what will you do for exercise, rest and recreation? If sport is where you have most of your friends, how will you keep in touch with them, or where will you seek further friendships? If sport was your livelihood, what will you do now for employment?

Rugby league international Brad Mackay provides a good example of how someone might retire well from professional sport. He was a Christian, a family man, and regular in church attendance. He prayed about the timing of his decision to retire, and had organized in advance to move into employment with the fire brigade, which he now describes as being like a family.

As is well known, recently retired sportspeople often experience some degree of depression. While the Christian athlete is able to deal with the challenges of retirement by doing the sorts of things described in this section, the non-believer can only do some of them. If we know non-Christians who are at this transition point, we have the opportunity to show them love and offer support. It may even be that they are ready to ponder the bigger questions of life. One sports chaplain commented to me that he felt that retired sportspeople were more open to spiritual matters than those who were currently playing.

Suggestion 4: Resolve to keep exercising

When we stop playing a sport, it is wise to keep exercising in some way if at all possible. Aside from the obvious physical benefits, regular exercise is usually good for our mental health, helps us to maintain a measure of discipline in our lives, and may keep us somewhat connected to a sporting existence.

Suggestion 5: Know that God still has important things for you to do

We may stop playing sport, but we never stop serving Christ. He has important things for us to do for the whole of our life. As Paul writes in Ephesians 2:10: "For we are God's handiwork, created in Christ Jesus to do good works, which God prepared in advance for us to do". God has good things for us to do—important things! As Nick Farr-Jones's and Brad Mackay's lives illustrate, retirement from sport is not the end; it is simply the transition point to what God has for us next.

And beyond...

Rugby union has often been described as 'the game they play in heaven'. No doubt, many would want to describe their favourite sport in similar terms. But it does raise an interesting question: Will we play sport in heaven?

The prophet Zechariah describes a heavenly scene in which "the city streets will be filled with boys and girls playing there" (Zech 8:5). While we know that the biblical descriptions of life in the new creation make liberal use of metaphors, it seems reasonable to assume that *play* (or something like it) might be just one of the many good things we will find in heaven. The Bible's descriptions of the new creation, such as in Revelation 21-22, suggest that there will be better versions of the good things we find on earth—for example, a better city, river, street and tree. This means it is at least possible that there will also be a better version of our favourite sport. Perhaps, with my new perfected and uninjured heavenly body (1 Cor

15:35-56), I will be able to consistently bowl a cricket ball that swings away from the batsman at great pace. And if there isn't sport in heaven, we will not miss it—something better will be in its place.

The point is that *this*—life in this world—is not all there is. The Christian can look forward to a far better existence in the future—with God, in the new creation. The young follower of Jesus who is passionate about their sport can look forward either to playing it, or participating in something a whole lot better, in eternity. And the older believer who recalls their athletic glories from bygone days, but whose body is now past that level of physical exertion, can look forward to a time when, in an ultimate sense:

> **They will soar on wings like eagles;**
> **they will run and not grow weary,**
> **they will walk and not be faint. (Isa 40:31b)**

The Christian sporting life is just an introduction to eternity.

A WORD FOR...

parents, coaches, teachers, referees, chaplains, ministers and spectators

> Start children off on the way they should go,
> and even when they are old they will not
> turn from it. (Proverbs 22:6)

///

Some of my earliest and happiest recollections relate to cricket—family games in the backyard, watching it on TV, and trips to the Sydney Cricket Ground (the 'SCG') to watch the Australian team in action. My parents loved the game. My father sat on the old SCG Hill during the infamous 'Bodyline' series of 1932-33. My mother recalled the likes of Keith Miller and Denis Compton playing at the Adelaide Oval just after the war. Given that I grew up in this sort of context, it wasn't long before I, too, was hooked. The cricket was constantly on our TV during the summer months, and when the Australian team was in England during the long nights of our winter, we would stay up late watching matches from exotic locations like Lord's, Headingley, Trent Bridge and The Oval.

As a boy, I played cricket on Friday afternoons for my primary school and on Saturday mornings for my local club. After a few seasons, my father put up his hand to score for my Saturday team. I was pleased—it was nice to have him there every weekend. Dad would regularly drive a carload of my teammates to and from games, often buying us ice-creams on the return journey regardless of whether we'd won or lost. I recall that, on one occasion, my friends and I were discussing some girls we knew from school. Later that day, my father, a humble man, indicated to me in a quiet but very clear way that, in his view, the way we had been talking about the girls had *not* been good. I've never forgotten this.

After a few years, my father took up the position of team coach. Dad wasn't overly athletic, but he was well-organized, fair and conscientious. He encouraged some of the other dads to be involved, made sure everyone had a good go at practice and in games, and treated everyone with both friendliness and respect. In the under-15s, with my father as coach, we won the local competition—something I remember fondly to this day.

Around this time, it was becoming clear that I was a player with potential, and I started to get picked in various representative sides. These games were sometimes on a Sunday. My parents, who had previously discouraged me from trying out for representative football because it clashed with church, allowed me to play representative cricket on those few Sundays over summer on the condition that I went to the evening church service with dad.

As I grew older and started to play grade cricket with men much older than me, my father was always ready to drive me to games anywhere in Sydney. And, if needed, he'd pick me up at the end of the day. He would talk to my teammates and their parents, wives and girlfriends. Although he was not particularly 'one of the boys', people always liked him.

Once it became apparent that I was not going to make it as a professional cricketer, I continued playing first grade cricket for about ten more seasons. I had moved away from home, but my team's home ground was near my parents' house. Mum would sometimes come to watch me play. Dad was even more regular. He would set himself up on the side of the ground opposite the clubhouse with a chair and a thermos of coffee. If we were bowling, he'd watch me with interest for an hour or two before heading home. If we were batting, I'd go around and sit with him while waiting for my own turn at the crease. We'd chat, sip our drinks, and watch the game.

My father fell ill during one of my final seasons in first grade. It proved to be leukaemia. He passed away not long after our last game. Hundreds attended his funeral. But one guy who could not make it was Mark—a member of our successful under-15s team from many years earlier. Mark wrote to me from New Zealand. He recalled how, after an end-of-year school speech day about 13 years earlier at which I had received an award or two, he'd said to my father, "Mr Liggins, you must be very proud of Stephen". Apparently, my father replied, "Mark, I'd be very proud of Stephen regardless of how well he went".

This chapter offers a few words for people who take various roles in relation to sport other than playing—parents, coaches and teachers, referees, chaplains, ministers, and spectators.

Each of these roles can be very important and influential, and each can be undertaken in a positive or negative way. At various times, my father filled three of them—in my view, very successfully. And throughout all of this he loved me, loved his cricket, and, most importantly, loved God. The way he filled these and the other roles he had in life contributed to the fact that I, his son, have filled those same roles that he did, and have added another—that of church minister. As the writer of Proverbs says, "Start children off on the way they should go, and even when they are old they will not turn from it" (Prov 22:6).[1]

Parents

Sport presents many wonderful opportunities, and some dangers, for the Christian parent. They can play sport with their children, watch sport with their children, and watch their children play sport. Parents may even find themselves coaching or managing their children's sporting teams. Time spent together in these ways can be highly bonding and very enjoyable, providing great teaching opportunities and creating special memories for all involved. As we saw in the previous chap-

---

[1] The book of Proverbs is an example of *wisdom literature*. This is a genre of writing that pondered the perplexities of life, and sought to provide instructions for successful living. It often set out wise sayings that described things that are usually true, rather than things which are true in every situation. So, for example, not every child of good Christian parents will grow up to be a Christian. However, ancient and modern wisdom indicates that the children of such parents are more likely to grow to be believers than the children of parents who do not follow Jesus.

ter, parents also face key decisions regarding their children's participation in sport.

As parents faced with navigating the ups and downs of the sporting world, what are some of the key truths to convey, opportunities to grasp, priorities to hold, and dangers to avoid?

God loves your children regardless

One important truth to convey to our children is that God loves them *regardless* of how they perform in their sport. It is very important that we help them to appreciate this, particularly given that we live in highly performance-based cultures. Former Oxford University rugby union player and now Church of England minister Rico Tice reflects on his time at boarding school. He recalls that the implicit message of the school was, in his words, "You're not good enough. You have to prove yourself."

"This created people who were unrelentingly achievement-driven", he says. Rico's experience would be far from unique. Thankfully, as Christians, we know that we do not have to perform to receive God's attention or earn his love. He has shown unconditional love to us in Christ (e.g. Rom 5:8). Our Christian children need to know that God loves them unconditionally, and that their identity is found in Christ, not in their sporting success.

You love your children regardless

We also need our children to know that *we* love them regardless of how they perform. This was what I believe my father was explaining to my friend Mark all those years ago.

One of the great dangers in sport is for parents to try to live out their own ambitions through their children. It is good and natural to feel pleasure as we watch our children compete—giving it a go, trying hard, working together with their teammates, displaying good sportsmanship, and perhaps even doing well. But it is not good to use our children to fulfil our dreams. The more we try to live out our dreams through our children, the more likely it is that we'll (perhaps inadvertently) apply pressure on them to perform, making them feel as though they can only earn our approval if their performances live up to our expectations. Leave your misplaced ambition behind, and love and support your children unconditionally as they make their own way in the world of sport.

Sport is part of the Christian life

A parent can encourage their Christian children to follow Jesus, and to see sport as part of their Christian life. We can do this by the example we set, and by the way that we speak about sport.

Hockey international Susie Harris grew up in a very positive spiritual environment. "My parents talked to me about Jesus and Christianity my whole life", she says. "We were a churchgoing family, and from a young age they encouraged me in the habit of personal Bible reading and prayer. They told me that as Christians we would often need to stand out as different from those around us. These foundations really helped me as I got older."

As parents, we can, in age-appropriate ways, seek to teach our children the principles outlined in this book. First and foremost, we must encourage them to become followers of Jesus and to put God first in every part of their lives. From there, we should teach them to thank God for the opportunity to play sport, to work hard at forming friendships, to encourage Christians in their sporting world, and to be a witness to non-Christians. We should train them to love others by, for example, doing their best, being a good team member, and showing good sportsmanship on and off the field.

It is also good to consider the sort of example we are setting. As in all areas of life, our encouragement will fall on deaf ears if we aren't providing a consistent model in our own behaviour. For example, what are we like on the sideline? A work colleague once described to me the words he heard a father shout to his son's football team as they ran onto the field: "Come on, Blahsville [an invented name]! Crush their spirits!"

Crush their spirits?! It was an under-10s game! Is that the sort of attitude we want to model?

A particular danger for parents is to accidentally convey to our kids that sport is more important than God. I remember a minister reflecting on whether his children saw him getting more excited about his favourite football team winning, or about someone becoming a Christian. It's a good question. Similarly, what do our children think is more important to us—having regular Christian fellowship, or regular sporting involvement? The words of Jesus in Mark 8:36 are relevant here: "What good is it for someone to gain the whole world, yet forfeit their soul?" My most heartfelt prayer for my children is that they grow up to be keen followers of Jesus, not that they be given every sporting opportunity available to them.

Opportunities to speak about life

Sport can give parents regular extended time with their children. Besides being very enjoyable, this can also give us the opportunity to speak to them, not only about sport, but also about life. Driving to and from games is a good time for this. And when our children are older and no longer live with us, sport may still provide a way for us to speak to them about important matters. Susie Harris told me that when she was living away from home or touring, her parents would often write her notes full of spiritual encouragement and life advice.

When our children are younger, sport can also give parents the opportunity to observe their offspring 'doing life' outside of the home. We don't usually get to see our kids at school, but we can observe them in action at sport. This provides the opportunity to affirm our kids when we see them behaving well, and to lovingly correct then when we see them going off course in some way (as my father did when he overheard that conversation about those girls from my school). The writer of Proverbs says, "Discipline your children, and they will give you peace; they will bring you the delights you desire" (Prov 29:17).

Relationships with other children and parents

An involvement with our children's sport not only gives us the opportunity to spend time with our kids; it also allows us to meet, befriend, enjoy, and hopefully have a positive influence on other people. It is said that "it takes a village to raise a child", and we can be part of that 'village' for other children. The sideline is also a great place to meet and befriend parents. The regular nature of much sport certainly allows for the development of these relationships.

///

So, how do you think you are going here? It doesn't take too much to make parents feel guilty about the inadequacies of their parenting. As Christians, it is good to know that we are saved by grace, that we can pray about our concerns, and that Jesus empathizes with our weaknesses (Heb 4:15). That said, why not resolve (with God's help) to make the most of relational opportunities that our children's sport brings?

Coaches and teachers

Sports coaches—whether professionals or volunteers—and physical education teachers can be highly influential members of our communities. Not only do they influence the athletic development of their charges, but they also have the opportunity to significantly influence their personal development.

As we saw in chapter 2, sport, historically, has been seen as an ideal way to build character and community and to develop leadership skills. This, I learned, was one of the biggest motivations for my under-16s football coach, whom we met in chapter 1. It was also a huge motivation for American football coach Kris Hogan, first mentioned in chapter 5. God clearly used Hogan to positively influence his team, their families, his school, his opponents—and, by virtue of his approach as exemplified in that famous game in 2008, people across the

United States of America and around the world.

As with all followers of Jesus, Christian coaches and teachers should make it their aim to love God and love their neighbour (Mark 12:30-31). Loving our neighbour means being committed to their good, so here are just a few ways in which a Christian coach or teacher might do this with respect to those they are coaching or teaching.[2]

Serve your team, don't use them

The Christian coach's brief is to develop their charges athletically and personally, and (depending on the context) spiritually. The focus is on what the coach can do for them, not what they can do for the coach. Jesus washed his disciples' feet to demonstrate the importance of leading by serving others (John 13:1-17). Serve your team; don't use them.

Let them enjoy themselves

In the vast majority of contexts, one of the main reasons people play sport is for enjoyment. Adults may refer to it as 'rest and recreation'; kids simply call it 'good fun'. Particularly when dealing with children, a good coach will focus on letting their charges enjoy themselves. Coaches can still work hard to develop skills and improve fitness, but, in ways appropriate to the age and level of seriousness. Promoting enjoyment should usually be a dominant aim. Even at the elite level, Christian

---

2 For convenience, throughout this section I will speak of coaches and their team or charges; teachers can simply substitute 'teacher' for 'coach' and 'students' for 'team' or 'charges'.

coaches can care for their athletes by encouraging them to keep things in perspective, and to enjoy and find satisfaction in their sport.

Develop their skills

This may seem obvious, but do your best to actually develop the sporting skills of your charges. If you are coaching a team of youngsters, some may end up playing your sport for a large part of their lives. Thus, what you teach them at an early age will influence them over the long term. Some may also have particular talent, and eventually manage to compete at an elite level. You may be one of the people who helped set them on their way. Of course, while volunteer coaches usually have limited time and expertise, there may be the chance to undertake a coaching course or do a little research. Other coaches can also be a great resource. However you approach it, developing your athletes' skills should help them to gain more from the sport.

Promote good character

One of the most common reasons that parents encourage their children to play sport is character development. But this is not just important for children. At whatever level you are coaching, think about how you can model and promote sportsmanship and good character. Not only is this consistent with Christian ethics; most people would like to see more sportsmanship in the world. Most sports contain prominent examples of people who participate in an arrogant, selfish and unsportsmanlike manner. The Christian coach can work to counteract their influence.

Treat them as individuals

Do your best to coach *all* people in your team or training group. Don't just focus on the talented athletes or the vocal people; make sure you assist the less talented and the quiet as well. Also, remember that everyone is different. Try to treat people as individuals, and do your best to take into account the different personalities and values of your charges. It is interesting to note that Eric Liddell's coach, Tom McKercher, does not appear to have discouraged Eric from prioritizing God over athletics.[3] As such, he had the joy of coaching an Olympic champion.

Encourage friendships

Friendships are one of the great things sport can foster. Accordingly, don't act against this by setting up unhealthy rivalries—whether within a team or training squad, between teams, or with other competitors. Healthy competition is fine, but make sure that it does not come at the cost of positive relationships.

Point people towards Christ

Finally, we always want to point people towards Christ in ways appropriate to our circumstances. How this might be done will vary from one coaching situation to the next. If you are coaching at a Christian school or in a churches' competition, it may be appropriate to take a very direct approach. You might pray with those you coach, and perhaps explicitly teach them about

---

3   Hamilton, *For the Glory*, pp. 41-4.

the gospel, the Christian life, and the intersection of sport and Christianity.

If, however, you are coaching in a secular context, you will need to be more circumspect. For example, if you are coaching a children's basketball team, the parents will be pleased if you teach them basketball and good character in an even-handed way, but some may be very unhappy if you turn it into a secret Sunday School class. That is quite reasonable on their part; they have put their children under your care to teach them basketball, not to turn them into Christians. Whatever the context, a Christian coach should pray for those they coach, coach well, and coach in a loving way. It should be fine to let players and parents know that you are a Christian or that you go to church, but leave it at that. People can join the dots and ask you about your faith if they are interested.

Referees and umpires

Referees and umpires also provide a great service to sport and the community. In most situations, a game or race depends on people being willing to officiate, and it is sometimes a thankless task. Christians can honour Christ by seeking to referee and umpire well, fairly, and in a way that shows genuine interest in and care for the players.

David Tyndall, former National Coordinator of Sports Chaplaincy Australia, played Sydney first grade rugby union for many years before becoming an International Sevens and grade referee. He suggests that referees should seek to be good "people managers" and that they should try to officiate in such a way as to "make the game work". They ought not to show favouritism, which is especially difficult when placed under enormous pressure by the players, the crowd, and (at the highest levels) the media.

Referees need to be people of the highest integrity. Such a person will almost always win the respect of others. In terms of seeking to point people towards Christ, similar principles would apply to referees as to coaches. Referee well, and you will not only promote a good game; you may also promote something far more important.

Chaplains

While sports chaplaincy is a great form of Christian ministry, what a chaplain actually does can often be something of a mystery. In most cases, the role of a sports chaplain is to provide pastoral support to athletes and club members, and to offer spiritual assistance where appropriate. This spiritual assistance may involve encouraging believers and talking with interested non-believers. Depending upon their qualifications, a chaplain might also be invited to conduct baptisms, weddings and funerals. They may be called upon when some tragedy strikes, such as when a club member is seriously injured or killed.

Graham Crew's ministry at the St George rugby league club in the 1990s is typical. A full-time Anglican minister, his chaplaincy role was part-time and voluntary. Graham would attend training, games, and some social events. He would call people when there was an injury or a significant life event and, when appropriate, would meet up with players to discuss spiritual issues. As described in chapter 6, Graham found himself sharing the gospel with both Brad Mackay and Jason Stevens, explaining the faith and answering their questions. When they became followers of Jesus, he helped to support and consolidate them in their new Christian lives.

At the top level of certain sports, Christian participants can often find it hard to attend church every week because of games and travel. In such circumstances, a chaplain can help provide much needed teaching, Bible study, prayer, support and guidance. When Linvoy Primus became a Christian during his time at Portsmouth FC, the club chaplain answered Linvoy's questions, urged him to seek to glorify God in his football, and encouraged him to pray for other footballers. During Linvoy's time at the club, he and the chaplain saw about five players become believers.

In the early days, sports chaplaincy focussed on elite sportspeople and clubs, but has moved more recently into local sports clubs as well. In many countries, there are umbrella organizations that oversee sports chaplaincy, recruiting chaplains and providing guidance and training. For example, Sports Chaplaincy Australia oversees most of this ministry in Australia, while Sports Chaplaincy UK serves the same role in the UK.

I asked a number of sports chaplains for their tips on what makes a good chaplain. Here are some of their key pieces of advice:

- » build good relationships with players, coaches and staff
- » be prayerful (and get people to pray for you)
- » be visible and take initiative
- » show grace, and point people to the gospel of grace

- » look for ways to provide practical help and assistance around the club
- » don't be a 'fan' (i.e. don't ask for selfies, autographs or freebies)
- » be patient, as the ministry can be very slow
- » while there are encouragements, be prepared for disappointments.

The ministry of a sports chaplain not only affects the athletes; it can also have a significant impact upon the chaplain and the chaplain's church. Graham Crew says that being a chaplain was great for him as a local pastor—it moved him out into the community as a representative for Christ. He also included people from his church, organizing for church members to pray for individual St George players and staff.

If you are not a chaplain but are interested, why not contact the relevant umbrella organization in your country and find out how you could be involved?

Ministers

Sport can provide something of a challenge for a local church minister. On the one hand, as we've seen throughout this book, sport is a good gift from God with so many potential benefits. On the other hand, Sunday sport (along with training or related travel) can keep some Christian sportspeople away from regular church attendance or from getting involved in church-based ministry. There are also the dangers of sports-related idolatrous attitudes and immorality. How might we respond to this situation? As a minister myself, here are a few suggestions for handling the opportunities and challenges.

Preach, pray and pastor

Whatever our situation, we need to keep our focus on preaching God's word, praying for our people, pastoring our people, and praying for and reaching out to the world. We will be concerned that our church fulfils the Great Commandments (Matt 22:37-39) and the Great Commission (Matt 28:18-20). We will encourage our people to engage in personal Bible reading and prayer, regular Christian fellowship, and Christian ministry.

When it comes to the specific issues around sport, it helps to familiarize ourselves with the Bible's teaching as it relates to sport, and with the many opportunities that sport provides for evangelism and discipleship (hopefully, this book has been some help in that regard). This will mean we are well placed to help our people think wisely about the sport-related issues in our culture, and to better assist sportspeople when they come to us for advice. Whatever situations we face, we should keep the gospel front and centre in our own thinking and our ministry, and help our people to see how the gospel shapes their thinking about sport.

Support Christian sportspeople

Consider some things the church can do to assist Christians who play, or would like to play, sport. For example, if it has the capacity, it is very helpful for a church to hold a Sunday afternoon or evening gathering to provide an alternative for those involved in Sunday morning sport, and to provide good opportunities for ministry during the week. Throughout my time playing first grade cricket, most games were on Saturdays, but there were usually about six to eight Sundays a year with games scheduled. This had little impact on me as the church service I was part of each week took place on a Sunday night, and I would simply attend after the game. In terms of ministry, I was involved with young adults' work which took place on weeknights rather than on Sunday mornings.

In addition to your formal ministries, your church could also organize flexible pastoral support for church members who are top-level sportspeople and who may find regular Sunday church attendance difficult. Pete Nicholas suggests connecting elite sportspeople with one or two church members, adding that it might even be a help if these people don't care too much about sport. Pete's wife, for example, meets regularly with one top-flight female athlete for fellowship and support. They don't talk about sport a lot when they get together; they simply meet as Christian women and seek to spur each other on in the Lord. This is the sort of ministry in which sports chaplains often engage, but there is no reason why a church cannot do it.

Spectators

Finally, let's briefly consider the lot of the Christian sports spectator. Interestingly, Oxford academic Robert Ellis asserts that people tend to play sport and watch sport for similar reasons. These reasons include simple enjoyment, rest and the relief of stress, social motives, enjoyment of competition and, less consciously, to establish and maintain an identity.[4] And here, as is the case with playing sport, we can do this in a spiritually positive or spiritually negative way.

Whether we are watching our children, our favourite club, our national team, or a local, national or international competition, it is possible to get great enjoyment out of watching sport. We might find it restful, stress-relieving, stimulating, inspiring and exciting. We can appreciate the great skill involved, the excitement of competition, and perhaps enjoy watching someone we know take part. There is also the camaraderie we can experience with our fellow spectators.

I recall being at the Sydney Olympic stadium in 2005 and seeing the Australian football team qualify for the World Cup Finals for the first time in 32 years. As an Australian fan, the excitement and tension of the game was incredible. When John Aloisi scored the winning goal in the penalty shootout, I, along with 90,000 other spectators, erupted from our seats and threw our arms into the air with a roar. I found myself hugging people I'd never met before. The excitement of it all remained with me for a few days.

Of course, I love watching my children play sport—seeing them doing their best, learning skills, having fun with friends, and doing something healthy is a delight. I also enjoy viewing sport on television; as a youngster, I often found it inspiring. Watching Dennis Lillee and Jeff Thomson, Australia's great fast bowlers from the mid-1970s, no doubt motivated me to become a fast bowler, leading to 25 years of competitive cricket

---

4   See Ellis, pp. 167-89, 250-7.

with all its associated benefits and blessings.

These days, when I get the chance to watch sport on television, I usually find it restful. Each year I look forward to lying on the couch and watching a few hours of cricket in the Boxing Day Test from Melbourne. After the busyness of the lead-up to Christmas, it is a very welcome way to wind down. I also often make a point of watching sport with my church and non-church friends. This can be a very enjoyable and productive way to spend time together.

I'm sure most people reading this book could identify with these sorts of pleasures and provide their own examples. As with playing sport, watching sport can be viewed as a good gift from God, to be received with thanksgiving. Don't forget to thank God for it.

But, sadly, like everything else, watching sport can be damaged by sin. Common mistakes are to obsess over sport, idolize sport, waste too much time watching sport, and to react poorly when sport does not go the way we would like it to. Sports watching can have its highly unpleasant side. Think of the amount of abuse and vitriol shouted from the sidelines and stands of sporting venues around the world. And watching sport sometimes has a horribly dark side, too—and it's not just violence between rival groups of fans. It has been reported that domestic violence in Glasgow doubles when Rangers play Celtic (two rival Glaswegian teams). A similar spike in domestic violence can be seen in New Zealand when the All Blacks (the national rugby team) are defeated.[5]

---

5   Ellis, p. 252.

English Christian writer, editor, and self-confessed sports nut Carl Laferton has reflected on the potentially idolatrous nature of watching sport. He writes: "I've tried to spot when I am enjoying sport as a good thing, given by the God who wants us to enjoy the world he's made us to live in; and when I am straying towards sport as a god thing, replacing God in my affections, capturing my excitement, leaving me feeling empty when we lose. I've asked the Spirit to prod me when I am beginning to define myself more in terms of my country-tribe or team-tribe than in terms of Jesus' tribe (he calls it the church)."[6]

Let's do whatever we can to ensure that our sports viewing is a spiritual plus rather than a spiritual minus.

---

[6] Carl Laferton, 'Last Night, We Won', *The Good Book Co. blog*, 12 July 2018: thegoodbook.com.au/blog/interestingthoughts/2018/07/12/last-night-we-won/.

A WORD ABOUT...

sport on Sundays, praying for victory, how much sport, and sports ministry

> And whatever you do, whether in word or deed, do it all in the name of the Lord Jesus, giving thanks to God the Father through him. (Colossians 3:17)

///

I've reached the final chapter of this book without having said anything about wrestling. Perhaps the time has come.

Wrestling is a combat sport in which two competitors fight by gripping each other using special holds. It can take many forms. There is, of course, professional wrestling, which is probably best regarded as highly skilful entertainment. Other forms include Greco-Roman and freestyle wrestling—both Olympic sports. In these versions, you win by pinning your opponent to the mat. You cannot win if you fail to pin them down. This chapter is a little like losing a wrestling match: it contains topics that I've failed to pin down.

Sport on Sunday

Well, here's an issue that's a big one for many people: Should Christians play sport on Sunday? It might be this very topic that has prompted you to look at this book, and this is the first section to which you have turned.

Today an increasing amount of sport—local, representative and professional—is being played on Sunday. But of course Sunday is also the day on which Christians have traditionally met together for Bible teaching, prayer and fellowship. So what happens when sport clashes with attendance at Sunday church? How should we think about this vexed issue?

What follows will necessarily be a simplified summary of various arguments, so apologies in advance if you do not think I have picked up the nuances of a particular position or addressed a specific question you would like answered.

The Bible makes it very clear that Christians should put the concerns of God first in their lives—that we must seek first the kingdom of God and his righteousness (Matt 6:33). As such, we need to devote ourselves to loving God with all our heart, soul, mind and strength, and loving our neighbour as ourselves (Mark 12:29-31). As part of this, meeting regularly with other Christians for Bible teaching, prayer and fellowship is clearly a biblical priority (Heb 10:25). We have also seen in this book that sport is a good gift from God with many potential benefits for the kingdom of God and for one's spiritual life.

I would suggest that there are four main positions held by Christians on the topic of playing sport on Sunday, each being held for a variety of reasons:

1. One should *never* play sport on a Sunday
2. It is okay to play sport on Sundays as long as it *does not interfere* with Sunday church attendance
3. It is okay to play sport on Sundays even if it *does interfere* with Sunday church attendance, *as long as* appropriate arrangements can be made to meet together regularly with other Christians for Bible teaching, prayer and fellowship
3. One can simply play sport on Sundays if one wishes and get to church and Christian fellowship if and when it happens to be convenient.

In my view, the fourth position is the easiest to rule out. It prioritizes sport over meeting together with God's people for Bible teaching, prayer and fellowship. Sport is not a biblical essential—while meeting together with other Christians is (Heb 10:25).[1] When it comes to deciding between the other three positions, people's views tend to be the result of their understanding of whether Sunday is the Sabbath, and/or the Lord's Day, and/or a day of rest, and/or the day for church. To understand these issues, we need to answer two questions:

1. Does the Bible say that Christians should meet on Sunday?

---

[1] To slightly nuance this last statement, there are a very small number of situations in which Christians may not be able to meet together with other believers—for example, in those countries where Christians are sometimes arrested for their faith and placed in solitary confinement. The idea is that we meet together with other believers if at all humanly possible.

2. Does the Bible say that Sunday is the Sabbath, or the Lord's Day, or a day of rest, such that playing sport on that day is precluded?

We will address each question in turn.

Should Christians meet together on Sundays?

While the Bible teaches that Christians should meet together regularly, and describes how Christians have met together regularly since the very beginning of the church (e.g. Acts 2:42-47), there is no biblical instruction suggesting that Christians should do this on a Sunday.

Having said that, the usual practice of Christians from earliest times has been to meet on a Sunday. We are told that when the apostle Paul was in Troas on his third missionary journey, "On the first day of the week [i.e. Sunday] we came together to break bread. Paul spoke to the people…" (Acts 20:7). Paul also seemed to know that the Corinthian church met regularly on Sundays (1 Cor 16:2).

Second-century Christian apologist Justin Martyr records that "on the day called Sunday, all who live in cities or in the country gather together to one place" where the Scriptures are read and taught, prayers are prayed, bread and wine is distributed, and money is collected.[2] Most Christians have met together on Sundays for two millennia, and today there are many good and practical reasons to do so—for example, most people have fewer work obligations on Sunday than on any

---

2 Justin Martyr, *First Apology*, 67, trans. A Roberts and J Donaldson: logoslibrary.org/justin/apology1/67.html.

other day of the week. Most churches have their main services on a Sunday.

Accordingly, while not a biblical mandate, it makes very good sense to meet together weekly with Christians on a Sunday unless there is a very good reason not to do so.

Does the Bible say that Sunday is the Sabbath, or the Lord's Day, or a day of rest, such that playing sport on that day is precluded?

While many Christians throughout history have answered this question in the affirmative, I would humbly submit that this position is not biblical. Here is a general historical summary of how God's people have approached this issue over the centuries:[3]

- » There is no particular evidence that Sunday was seen as a 'day of rest' in the earliest centuries of the Christian church.
- » In AD 321, the Emperor Constantine legislated that people should rest from work on Sunday. Despite Constantine's enactment, there were few ecclesiastical attempts to prohibit Sunday work until the 6th century, and Sunday rest was not observed even in monastic life.
- » Resting on Sundays came to the fore in the medieval period.

---

[3] The historical summary is based on DA Carson (ed.), *From Sabbath to Lord's Day: A biblical, historical and theological investigation*, Zondervan, Grand Rapids, 1982. See especially the chapters by RJ Bauckham, pp. 221-341, and AT Lincoln, pp. 343-412.

- » In the 16th century, the reformer Martin Luther reacted against the strict resting idea.
- » In the 17th century, the Puritans liked the idea of resting from work on Sundays, and added that Sundays were not a day for sports, pastimes, worldly words and worldly thoughts. Sunday was a day for worship, piety, mercy and charity.

Today there are a variety of views, which might conveniently be divided into two main positions:
1. Sunday is the Lord's Day—like a Christian Sabbath—and God's people should rest on this day. (For some, but not others, rest would include not playing sport.)
2. Christ fulfils the Old Testament law, and there is therefore no biblical requirement to rest on Sunday—although it is good and wise to get regular rest.

I believe the Bible teaches the second position.

In the Old Testament, God told the Israelites to rest one day each week. The fourth commandment reads:

> "Remember the Sabbath day by keeping it holy. Six days you shall labour and do all your work, but the seventh day is a sabbath to the LORD your God. On it you shall not do any work, neither you, nor your son or daughter, nor your male or female servant, nor your animals, nor any foreigner residing in your towns." (Exod 20:8-10)

But there is no equivalent New Testament teaching about a Sabbath Day or a Lord's Day as a day of rest. Yes, the apostle John refers to "the Lord's Day" in Revelation 1:10, which seems to be a reference to Sunday—and as we've already seen, the earliest Christians met together on Sundays. But this does not mean they were *required* to meet on Sundays as a matter of *obedience*. And while the New Testament speaks about the idea of 'rest', it is not with reference to a certain day of the week, but rather describes the 'rest' that Jesus offers his people (e.g. Matt 11:28; Heb 3:7-4:11).[4]

So in summary, I would argue that there is no biblical requirement to meet with other Christians specifically on a Sunday for Bible teaching, prayer and fellowship. That said, it is clearly a biblical priority that we meet regularly to do these things. Since most churches hold their main church meetings on a Sunday, I would strongly suggest that, wherever possible, every Christian should meet with God's people on a Sunday unless there is a *good kingdom-of-God reason* not to do so. In this case, other arrangements should be made for regular Bible teaching, prayer and fellowship.

What might constitute a *good kingdom-of-God reason* to miss Sunday church for sport?

This is a good question. A person will best be able to make a good decision here when their relationship with God is strong, when they prayerfully and biblically think through the issue, and when they consult with other wise Christians. It would also be a very good idea to discuss the matter with the minister of your church.

---

4 The 'rest' described in Matthew 11:28 seems to have both a present and future aspect, while the 'rest' of Hebrews 3:7-4:11 appears to emphasize a Christian's eternal rest.

So what might a 'good kingdom of God reason' entail? It is difficult to lay down strict guidelines, but some situations might include: where playing sport is a person's job (or will potentially be their job) and they consider it important that they pursue it; or where a person considers that it is important that they are a Christian witness in that particular sporting community. There could be other reasons as well.

If you do decide to participate in Sunday sport, let me emphasize again that you should prioritize making alternative arrangements for regular Bible teaching, prayer and fellowship. Where possible, all Christians should also engage in some form of Christian ministry. Consider how you can serve your church and the world, and build this into your weekly schedule. Use your gifts and play your part in 'the body of Christ' (1 Cor 12:4-27). If you are a church leader, do whatever you realistically can to help the athlete achieve these goals.

Finally, it will be helpful to make it clear to others, in whatever way may be appropriate, that while you may be playing sport on Sundays, you consider your relationship with God to be the top priority in your life.

Praying for victory?

We often see sportspeople, either by themselves or with teammates, praying before, during, and after games. American football quarterback Tim Tebow would famously drop down onto one knee with his head bowed and his arm resting on the bent knee to pray.⁵ Of course it is good to immerse all aspects of our lives, including our sport, in prayer. And amongst the many things that a sportsperson might consider praying about, victory in a sporting contest is certainly one of them.

But should we pray that we'll win? Sure, we know other things are far more important than the result of a game or race, but is it okay to pray for victory?

The Bible tells us that we can pray about anything:

> **Do not be anxious about anything, but in every situation, by prayer and petition, with thanksgiving, present your requests to God. And the peace of God, which transcends all understanding, will guard your hearts and your minds in Christ Jesus. (Phil 4:6-7)**

Accordingly, we can pray about *anything* from finding a spot in a car park, to victory in sport, to worldwide Christian revival. But while we can pray about anything, and Scripture does give us assurances that God will answer certain prayers in certain ways (e.g. for forgiveness of sins in 1 John 1:9), it never says that he will do *whatever* we ask. This is quite a relief—imagine if God did *whatever* we asked! Rather, whatever the topic, all our prayers are subject to God's will (1 John 5:14).

The Lord's Prayer contains a petition that God's "will be done" (Matt 6:10). When Jesus prayed in the Garden of Gethsemane about something infinitely more important than a sporting contest—asking that the 'cup' of suffering (i.e. his

---

5   This posture is now known as *tebowing*: wikipedia.org/wiki/Tim_Tebow#"Tebowing". There is even a website where people can send in photos of themselves tebowing: tebowing.com!

A WORD ABOUT...

looming crucifixion in which he would bear our sins in his body) be taken from him—he adds, "Yet not as I will, but as you will" (Matt 26:39).

Given this truth, it makes sense to acknowledge that all our petitions are subject to God's will. So if we are keen to win some sporting contest, it is entirely appropriate to pray about it, but to acknowledge that ultimately we want God's will to be done. We might pray along the following lines:

> Dear God,
>
> I would really like to win this game/race, and I pray that you would give me victory if it is your will. Please help me to do my best. And whatever happens, help me to glorify you before, during, and after the contest, whatever the result.
>
> Amen.

Of course, there are many other things we could pray about with respect to a sporting contest—for example, we might thank God for allowing us to participate, we might pray for opportunities to share our faith, and we might ask that God would keep us and others safe. If we are *only* praying for victory, it is probably a sign that our priorities are wrong.

How much sport should we play (if any)?

'Rampaging' Roy Slaven and HG Nelson are Australian comedians who regularly hold forth on a plethora of sports-related topics. Amongst a host of oft-repeated sayings they have inserted into contemporary Australian discourse is the assertion that "too much sport is never enough". Could that possibly be true? After all, this book has argued that sport is a good gift from God, and has set out its various physical, mental, social and spiritual benefits. Is it ever possible to have too much of a good thing?

When considering our level of commitment to sport, we need to reflect on ourselves and our circumstances in the light of God's concerns for us and our world. The stronger our relationship with God, the better we will be able to do this.

Should we play sport at all?

No-one *has* to play sport. There is no biblical injunction instructing us to do so. People have different interests and inclinations, and many will simply decide not to take part. That's pretty straightforward!

But there are also circumstances in which a Christian who likes playing sport may be better off not participating. For example, they may find that, with various other responsibilities—for example, family, church and work—they simply do not have time. This situation may persist for a few years—for example, while the children are young—or it may be lifelong—for example, where a person has to work two jobs, or has to care for a dependent family member.

There are also certain circumstances where a Christian who likes sport, has time to participate, and may even be very talented would be better to abstain from sport—at least for a time. For example, consider a person who is simply unable to control their behaviour either on the field or off the field. If the person is aware of the problem and has taken genuine steps to change but is simply unable to do so, it would be better for them to discontinue that sport rather than to dishonour God on a weekly basis. It may be that at a later date, with increased Christian maturity, they will be able to return to the sport with greater self-control. Other options might be to play with a different group of people, or to try a different sport. I would think that in most circumstances, with the work of God's Spirit and the support of friends, we should be able to grow in godliness both on and off the field and continue enjoying our sport. But if we simply cannot, drastic action may be required.[6]

If we play sport, how much should we play?

Is it possible, despite Roy and HG's assertion, to play (or watch) too much sport? In thinking about this we need to consider our reasons for playing sport, our personal circumstances, and our responsibilities in the light of scriptural concerns and priorities.

As we have seen in this book, there are many good reasons for playing sport. I would suggest that if we are playing purely for enjoyment, rest or recreation, we may devote a certain amount of time to it. If we are also playing for reasons of health, outreach or spiritual encouragement, we may devote more time to it. If sport is our profession, or we hope it may become our profession, we will devote more time to it yet again.

The amount of sport we play needs to fit in with our cir-

---

[6] See, for example, Mark 9:43-48. Jesus is not advocating that we literally cut off our hand or foot, or gouge out our eye, but is teaching (in a memorable way) that if something causes us to sin, serious action may be required.

cumstances and responsibilities as Christians in God's world. We live in the "last days" between Jesus' first coming and his return.[7] We must seek to bring glory to God in the way that we live. This will involve loving God and others in the ways described in the Bible. There is our relationship with God to foster, fellowship to be had, Christians to love and build up in the faith, non-believers to love and point towards Jesus, a world with needs to be met, and good things in this world to thank God for and enjoy. We have responsibilities to our family, our church and our friends. We need to organize our life in such a way that we are living wisely in the light of these concerns.[8]

Sports ministry

So let's finish this chapter by thinking again about sport and gospel ministry. As we have seen, sport provides so many great opportunities for highly profitable Christian ministry. This can include informal personal ministries such as discipleship and evangelism and organized personal ministries such as sports chaplaincy. But sport can also be used for ministry purposes in

---

7 See, for example, Acts 2:17, 2 Tim 3:1, Hebrews 1:1-2, and James 5:3.
8 A very stimulating book by Mikey Lynch entitled *The Good Life in the Last Days: Making good choices when the time is short* (Matthias Media, 2018) helpfully addresses the question of how to enjoy the good things in this world, while at the same time being devoted to loving God and others in this fallen and needy world. He argues that we need to spiritually reflect on ourselves and our circumstances, and seeks to show that "sacrificing for the gospel is how to live well in God's good-but-fallen-creation in these last days" (p. 23). What this looks like in practice will vary from person to person.

more formalized, large-scale ways. Let's consider two prominent examples: church-based ministries, and organizations that exist for the very purpose of engaging in sports ministry.

Church-based sports ministries

Rico Tice, former Oxford University rugby player, sports fan, and now a minister at a large central London church, describes how his church seeks to reach out to the community by providing various weekly, no-cost, 'non-committal' sports—around 14 sports, in fact, including touch rugby, ultimate frisbee, tennis, table tennis, a running club, rock climbing, golf, and five-a-side football. "While many people in London love sport, they are time-poor", Rico explains. "If there is a sport for which they don't have to pay, and for which they don't have to turn up every week, many will be very keen to participate when they can. They are aware that the church is putting it on for them, and are grateful."

Rico says that each sports venture is marked by the 'four Ps'—*prayer*, being *prepared* to fail, being run by a *passionate* individual in the church, and *preaching* Christ. Each sport also has a clear 'gospel pathway'. At the touch rugby, for example, church members are encouraged to build relationship with non-church members. As appropriate, they look for opportunities to invite their non-church friends to read the Bible with them, or to invite them to a non-threatening event like a Christmas Carols service. The next step might be to invite them to a *Christianity Explored* course, or to church itself. "Each term," says Rico, "our *Christianity Explored* course contains people who have been contacted in this way". Rico also regularly gives sports-based gospel talks to groups of people contacted through the sports ministry.

While few churches could approach the scale of sports ministry being offered by Rico's church, perhaps yours could consider any or some of the following: forming sports teams, running fitness classes, offering a sports-focused outreach meeting with a guest speaker, holding a sports event (e.g. a golf day), running an outreach activity associated with a major sporting event (e.g. the Olympics or a significant final), or perhaps even incorporating sports facilities into your next church building project as a way of forming community contacts. If you have a particular passion for sport, perhaps you could speak to your minister and offer to lead the way in trying one of these activities.

Sports ministry organizations

The other big area of organized sports ministry comes from parachurch ministries that exist for this very purpose. As we noted in chapter 2, the 20th century saw the growth of Christian sports organizations that aim to help Christian athletes to stand firm *in* their faith and to reach out *with* their faith. This has been particularly prominent in the United States, with large ministries such as Sports Ambassadors, the Fellowship of Christian Athletes, and Athletes in Action. Christians in Sport commenced in the UK in the 1970s, and many countries have niche sports ministry organizations (e.g. Christian Surfers Australia) and groups that promote and oversee sports chaplaincy.[9]

Some sports ministries are national in focus, while others are international. One woman who has served in both contexts is former hockey player Jill Ireland, whom we met in chapter 6. After becoming a Christian and finishing her university studies, Jill commenced work with Christians in Sport—a ministry with which she served for nine years. Near the end of her time with this ministry, Jill started to seriously consider the possibility of serving God cross-culturally, and undertook two years of Bible college training. She eventually connected with the mission agency Serving in Mission (SIM) and their sports ministry called Sports Friends. Sports Friends seeks to train and equip leaders in local churches to make disciples of Jesus through sports ministry.

Jill has now served for a number of years with Sports Friends in South-East Asia, and quotes some impressive statistics about the work of this organization: "There are currently over 10,000 coaches in over 8,000 churches in 14 countries, ministering to 250,000 young people every week through church-centred sports ministry initiatives. Thousands of young people have come to faith in Jesus, their families and communities have been impacted, and hundreds of new churches have been planted using sport."

Clearly, sport can be used very effectively for outreach and discipleship.

---

9 While Christians in Sport UK encourages elite athletes (and athletes of all levels) to testify to their teammates and colleagues, it does not currently provide elite athletes as speakers for public events.

Conclusion

Sport is great—but there is something far greater. Betty Cuthbert was the golden girl of Australian athletics in the 1950s and 60s. To this day, she has won more athletics gold medals than any other Australian Olympian. At the 1956 Games in Melbourne, she won the 100 metres and 200 metres, and anchored the victorious Australian women's 4 x 100 metres relay team to another gold. Eight years later in Tokyo, she capped off her Olympic career with a victory in the 400 metres.

In the years that followed, Betty developed multiple sclerosis. But, far more importantly, she became a keen Christian. When I spoke with her a few years back, I found her to be a very encouraging and positive person. "I might have won four gold medals," she told me, "but the greatest thing is to know that everyone is a winner when they accept Jesus Christ into their life".

CONCLUSION

So whether you eat or drink or whatever you do, do it all for the glory of God.
(1 Corinthians 10:31)

///

The Sporting Life was a famous sports-themed British newspaper that was first published in 1859. Charles Dickens enthusiastically described himself as "a humble disciple" of the publication, while the Queen Mother once remarked: "Of course I read *The Sporting Life*."[1]

'The good life' is a phrase often used to describe the life that one would like to live. So popular is the idea that it has been used as the title for films, television series, books and songs.[2] This book is called *The Good Sporting Life* because it seeks to describe 'the good life' that one can strive to live in the popular area of sport. As we have seen, such a life needs to be part of a life lived for God.

The Sporting Life newspaper had a long and turbulent his-

---

1 James Lambie, *The Story of Your Life: A History of 'The Sporting Life' Newspaper (1859-1998)*, Matador, Leicester, 2010, p. 3.
2 See wikipedia.org/wiki/The_Good_Life.

tory, finally drawing to a close in 1998. Like that newspaper, the life of the sports-playing Christian will certainly have its ups and downs as we seek to embrace sport's intrinsic and instrumental values and resist the associated dangers of idolatry and immorality. Hopefully, if you have read this far—whatever your interest in sport—you feel better equipped to think about and interact with sport 'Christianly', such that it is a plus and not a minus for your spiritual life and for the kingdom of God.

Of course, the only *true* good life—the good life that we were created to live—is lived as we follow Jesus. Many contemporary ideas about what constitutes a 'good life' focus merely on our earthly life, but the Christian sportsperson has a much grander vision. As the apostle Paul writes near the end of his life:

> I have fought the good fight, I have finished the race, I have kept the faith. Now there is in store for me the crown of righteousness, which the Lord, the righteous Judge, will award to me on that day—and not only to me, but also to all who have longed for his appearing. (2 Tim 4:7-8)

Thanks to the incredible grace of God, we look forward to an eternity with God in the new heavens and new earth (Rev 21:1) where we will be with God and his people—including Eric Liddell, Betty Cuthbert, CT Studd, and the full host of Christian sporting luminaries. This is what awaits us after the final whistle, after stumps are drawn, at the race's end.

In the meantime, to slightly amend 1 Corinthians 10:31: "So whether you eat or drink *or play sport* or whatever you do, do it all for the glory of God."

ACKNOWLEDGEMENTS

///

This book could never have been written without the generous support and assistance of many people. I would particularly like to thank Anglican Churches Springwood for allowing me time off to write another book; Simon Pillar for his encouragement and very practical support; Lisa Neale and especially Geoff Robson for their fine editing work; and Tony Payne, Ian Carmichael, Emma Thornett, Georgia Condie, and the rest of the team at Matthias Media.

I am very grateful to those people who generously gave their time to be interviewed by me in preparation for writing this book: Jonathan Buckley, Ron Cardwell, Elizabeth Chambers, Nick Colyer, Graham Crew, Ben Cullen, Graham Daniels, Robert Ellis, Nick Farr-Jones, Simon Flinders, Debbie Flood, Cayley Hamilton, Susie Harris, Jill Ireland, Justine Jenner, Eddie and Sally Kopiec, Brad Mackay, Simon Manchester, Pete Nicholas, Ashley Null, Laurance Ollerton, Linvoy Primus, Priscilla Ruddle, Daniel Sams, Dave Simmons, Melinda Storm, Rico Tice, David Tyndall, Stuart Weir, Eloise Wellings, Andrew Wingfield Digby, Jules Wilkinson, and Steve Young. I really enjoyed meeting these people and/or interacting with them online. It was very encouraging. I also appreciate those people I interviewed back when I was writing articles for *Southern Cross Newspaper* from 1993 to 2001: Brian Booth, Stephen Carr, Betty Cuthbert, Wes Hall, Shaun Pollock, Darren Smith, Jason Stevens, and Paul Stevens.

A big thank you to the team at Christians in Sport in the United Kingdom who assisted me in a variety of ways, as well as to the Pillars, the Tooheys, and especially the Browns for providing me with accommodation for the fortnight when I was working on the book in England. I have also benefited greatly from the insights in a number of books and articles on Christianity and sport that I read (and have often cited) while writing this book. Also, three cheers again to Wikipedia—a very helpful resource.

As with my last book, I am especially thankful for the support of my family—my two children, Bill and Charlotte (who would prefer that I was writing about megalodons or unicorns), and most especially my wife, Shareen, who continues to be an unending source of encouragement to my writing, as well as in the rest of my life!

And finally, as always, I am most grateful to our great and loving God—who created, sustains and saves us, and who gave us the ingenuity to create sport, and the brains and bodies to play it. To God be the glory!!

ABOUT THE AUTHOR

///

Stephen Liggins has worked as a lawyer and in the media and, when younger, almost become a professional cricketer. These days he serves as a pastor at a church in Sydney, is a visiting lecturer at Sydney Missionary and Bible College, and writes Christian books and articles. He is the author of *Travelling the World as Citizens of Heaven*. Stephen was and is a keen sportsman—currently participating in masters' athletics with a focus on the throwing events—and over the years has thought deeply about how sport interacts with his Christian faith. He also enjoys movies, reading, and reminiscing about his backpacking days. He is married with two children and lives in Sydney's Blue Mountains.

Feedback on this resource

We really appreciate getting feedback about our resources—not just suggestions for how to improve them, but also positive feedback and ways they can be used.

You can send feedback to us via the 'Feedback' menu in our online store, or write to us at info@matthiasmedia.com.au.

matthiasmedia

Matthias Media is an evangelical publishing ministry that seeks to persuade all Christians of the truth of God's purposes in Jesus Christ as revealed in the Bible, and equip them with high-quality resources, so that by the work of the Holy Spirit they will:

- abandon their lives to the honour and service of Christ in daily holiness and decision-making
- pray constantly in Christ's name for the fruitfulness and growth of his gospel
- speak the Bible's life-changing word whenever and however they can—in the home, in the world and in the fellowship of his people.

Our resources range from Bible studies and books through to training courses, audio sermons and children's Sunday School material. To find out more, and to access samples and free downloads, visit our website:

www.matthiasmedia.com

How to buy our resources

1. Direct from us over the internet:
   - in the US: www.matthiasmedia.com
   - in Australia: www.matthiasmedia.com.au

2. Direct from us by phone: please visit our website for current phone contact information.

3. Through a range of outlets in various parts of the world. Visit **www.matthiasmedia.com/contact** for details about recommended retailers in your part of the world.

4. Trade enquiries can be addressed to:
   - in the US and Canada: sales@matthiasmedia.com
   - in Australia and the rest of the world: sales@matthiasmedia.com.au

---

Register at our website for our **free** regular email update to receive information about the latest new resources, **exclusive special offers**, and free articles to help you grow in your Christian life and ministry.

Also by Stephen Liggins

Travelling the World as Citizens of Heaven

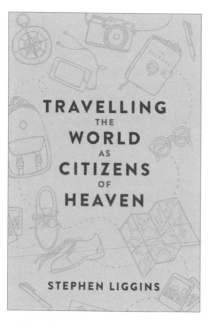

God's world is an amazing place. It boasts an incredible diversity of people, places, cultures, wildlife, and landscapes. And these days more and more people are heading off to travel or live overseas to experience it.

But as we walk through the airport on our way to becoming citizens of the world, is there anything that marks Christians out as different? What does it mean to travel the world as people whom the apostle Paul describes as 'citizens of heaven' (Phil 3:20)? How can we plan ahead to make our time overseas a positive rather than a negative for our spiritual life?

Author, pastor and experienced traveller, Stephen Liggins is your guide to thinking wisely and biblically about the what, why and how of overseas travel as a Christian.

Travelling the World as Citizens of Heaven is a must-read for just about any believer with a passport.

For more information or to order contact:

Matthias Media
Email: sales@matthiasmedia.com.au
www.matthiasmedia.com.au

Matthias Media (USA)
Email: sales@matthiasmedia.com
www.matthiasmedia.com

Also from Matthias Media

The Good Life in the Last Days
Making choices when the time is short
By Mikey Lynch

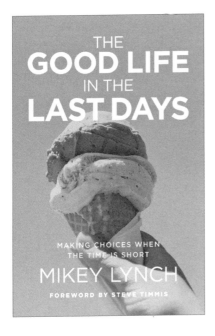

Do you feel the tension between living the good life and dying to self?

You know Jesus calls you to take up your cross and follow him, sacrificing yourself to serve in his vital gospel mission.

But you also know the heart of the gospel message is grace and freedom, and enjoying God's abundant generosity. Quite possibly you also know the horror stories of some burned out Christians, as well as the frustrating stories of those who just don't seem at all 'switched on' to the mission.

In *The Good Life in the Last Days* Mikey Lynch helps you:

- zoom in and take a close look at the hard sayings of Jesus and the apostles
- zoom out to look at the full counsel of God
- discover a joyful wisdom (beyond simplistic clichés) that shows you how to live the good life in the last days.

FOR MORE INFORMATION OR TO ORDER CONTACT:

Matthias Media
Email: sales@matthiasmedia.com.au
www.matthiasmedia.com.au

Matthias Media (USA)
Email: sales@matthiasmedia.com
www.matthiasmedia.com

Also from Matthias Media

Guidance and the Voice of God
by Phillip D Jensen and Tony Payne

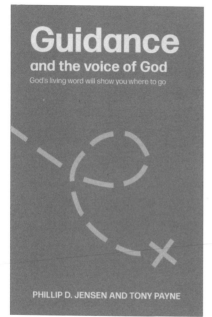

How do I know what God wants me to do? How can I make decisions that are in line with his will? If God still speaks, will I recognize his voice?

These are important questions, and many Christians grapple with them.

Guidance and the Voice of God charts a way through these often confusing issues, and shows how for those who have ears to hear, God is still speaking loud and clear through his Son.

For more information or to order contact:

Matthias Media
Email: sales@matthiasmedia.com.au
www.matthiasmedia.com.au

Matthias Media (USA)
Email: sales@matthiasmedia.com
www.matthiasmedia.com

Also from Matthias Media

Right Side Up
by Paul Grimmond

"I set out to write a book for new Christians, to explain what it means to be a Christian and what the lifelong adventure of following Jesus is like. But I soon realized that what Jesus wants to say to a new Christian is really the same thing he wants to keep saying to the seasoned saint: "Whoever loses his life for my sake will find it". My prayer is that this book will persuade you of the truth of those words, and help you live like you believe them. It's a book for the brand new Christian that should challenge every believer, whether you've been following Jesus for five minutes or fifty years."—Author, Paul Grimmond

For more information or to order contact:

Matthias Media
Email: sales@matthiasmedia.com.au
www.matthiasmedia.com.au

Matthias Media (USA)
Email: sales@matthiasmedia.com
www.matthiasmedia.com